BEETHOVEN'S
Symphony No. 9

Oxford KEYNOTES
Series Editor   KEVIN C. KARNES

Oxford KEYNOTES

BEETHOVEN'S
Symphony No. 9

ALEXANDER REHDING

Oxford University Press is a department of the University of Oxford. It furthers
the University's objective of excellence in research, scholarship, and education
by publishing worldwide. Oxford is a registered trade mark of Oxford University
Press in the UK and certain other countries.

Published in the United States of America by Oxford University Press
198 Madison Avenue, New York, NY 10016, United States of America.

Library of Congress Cataloging-in-Publication Data
Names: Rehding, Alexander author.
Title: Beethoven's Symphony no. 9 / Alexander Rehding.
Description: New York, NY : Oxford University Press, [2018] |
Series: Oxford keynotes | Includes bibliographical references and index.
Identifiers: LCCN 2017023667 | ISBN 9780190299699 (hardcover : alk. paper) |
ISBN 9780190299705 (pbk. : alk. paper)
Subjects: LCSH: Beethoven, Ludwig van, 1770–1827.
Symphonies, no. 9, op. 125, D minor.
Classification: LCC ML410.B42 R43 2018 | DDC 784.2/184—dc23
LC record available at https://lccn.loc.gov/2017023667

9 8 7 6 5 4 3 2 1
Paperback printed by Webcom, Inc., Canada
Hardback printed by Bridgeport National Bindery, Inc., United States of America

Series Editor's
INTRODUCTION

OXFORD KEYNOTES REIMAGINES THE canons of Western music for the twenty-first century. With each of its volumes dedicated to a single composition or album, the series provides an informed, critical, and provocative companion to music as artwork and experience. Books in the series explore how works of music have engaged listeners, performers, artists, and others through history and in the present. They illuminate the roles of musicians and musics in shaping Western cultures and societies, and they seek to spark discussion of ongoing transitions in contemporary musical landscapes. Each approaches its key work in a unique way, tailored to the distinct opportunities that the work presents. Targeted at performers, curious listeners, and advanced undergraduates, volumes in the series are written by expert and engaging voices in their fields, and will therefore be of significant interest to scholars and critics as well.

In selecting titles for the series, Oxford Keynotes balances two ways of defining the canons of Western music: as lists of works that critics and scholars deem to have articulated key moments in the history of the art, and as lists of works that comprise the bulk of what consumers listen to, purchase, and perform today. Often, the two lists intersect, but the overlap is imperfect. While not neglecting the first, Oxford Keynotes gives considerable weight to the second. It confronts the musicological canon with the living repertoire of performance and recording in classical, popular, jazz, and other idioms. And it seeks to expand that living repertoire through the latest musicological research.

Kevin C. Karnes
Emory University

CONTENTS

ABOUT THE
COMPANION WEBSITE

OXFORD UNIVERSITY PRESS HAS created a website to accompany *Beethoven's Symphony no. 9* that features a variety of related multimedia materials, including audio clips for all in-text musical examples. Many of these resources are integral to the volume itself or provide needed and useful context. As with all of the websites for Oxford Keynotes volumes, the reader is encouraged to take advantage of this valuable online information to expand their experience beyond the print book in hand. Examples available online are indicated in the text with Oxford's symbol ⯈.

www.oup.com/us/bsn9
Username: Music1
Password: Book5983

The reader is invited to explore the full catalog of Oxford Keynotes volumes on the series homepage.
www.oup.com/us/oxfordkeynotes

ACKNOWLEDGMENTS

T HIS BOOK WAS IN the making for both a fairly short and a very long time. While the writing process was relatively swift, this manuscript, like every book manuscript, contains hidden personal histories that can stretch back years, in some cases decades. It is a pleasure—tinged with nostalgia, to be sure—to cast the mind's eye back to these times, to remember that a book is not only a product but also a process, and to thank the many friends and colleagues without whom this book simply would not have happened.

It would not be too hard to bookend this project between the fall of 2002, specifically a party with the Princeton music graduate students when Greg Spears first introduced me to Leif Inge's 9 *Beet Stretch* (then still in its first online incarnation, chopped up into one-hour blocks), and January 2017, when Leif Inge patiently and graciously answered some last-minute questions I still had about his work. To both I am very grateful, as I am to my other composer friends who continually clean out my ears, especially Trevor Bača, Betsey Biggs, Ian Power, and Omar Thomas.

Or, for an alternative personal trajectory, we could start with the seminar course Signal to Noise, co-taught by Branden Joseph and Thomas Levin, that I audited in the spring of 2003, which first opened my eyes and ears to the field of media studies and put me on a path that led me to this book. Much more recently, friends and colleagues, including Andrea Bohlman, Kiene Brillenburg Würth, Seth Kim Cohen, Sybille Krämer, Deirdre Loughridge, Sander van Maas, Peter McMurray, John Durham Peters, and Jonathan Sterne, have deepened my appreciation and understanding of sound and its media.

A special shout-out goes to the brilliant group of students who gave me the opportunity to try out some ideas in the context of a graduate seminar I taught in the fall of 2015 at Harvard, especially Henry Burnam, who became fascinated by the bassoon in Beethoven flash mobs. Jeremy Eichler, Jonathan Service, Will Cheng, and Evander Price—Go Chronocritics!—always keep me on my toes. Thanks go to my Beethovenian friends, Daniel Chua, John Deathridge, Tom Kelly, Lewis Lockwood, Edgardo Salinas, and especially Nicholas Mathew, who organized a memorable symposium at Berkeley, Beyond the Valley of the Ninth, in 2015 and to whom I am indebted in so many ways. Kevin Karnes encouraged me in 2013 to write this book, and Suzanne Ryan shepherded it through the various stages of production. Together they are the alpha and the omega that made this book happen, from beginning to end.

Much of the writing happened during a sabbatical year at the Radcliffe Institute for Advanced Study in 2014–15. I am grateful for the support that I received during that time, and I cherish the stimulating conversations with fellows and colleagues, which imprinted themselves, directly or indirectly, onto the pages of this book. I am grateful I had the opportunity to revisit research done previously, in the context of this book, to dig deeper into some of the questions raised there, especially in my articles "'Ode to Freedom': Bernstein's Ninth at the Berlin Wall," *Beethoven Forum* 11, no. 1 (2005): 33–46, and "The Discovery of Slowness," in Sander van Maas, ed., *Thresholds of Listening* (New York: Fordham University Press, 2015), 206–225. Etha Williams and Grace Edgar provided invaluable help during the final editing process, and the production team at Oxford University Press sprinkled a generous portion of magic fairy dust on the manuscript that turned my plain Word document into an actual book.

The administrative team at Harvard's Music Department, around Christopher Danforth, Eva Kim, Karen Rynne, and Nancy Shafman, are peerless, as are the wonderful staff of the Loeb Music Library. They have left their imprint on the manuscript in countless ways. And at home, Bevil Conway and our twins Emmy and Benjamin remind me on a daily basis why we have chosen to look ahead to the future with optimism.

BEETHOVEN'S
Symphony No. 9

CHAPTER 1

BEETHOVEN'S NINTH
FOR A NEW MILLENNIUM

Persse McGarrigle, the ambitious graduate student from David Lodge's humorous British academic novel *Small World* (1984), is peeved: a senior scholar by the name of Professor Robin Dempsey has suggested that McGarrigle's master's thesis, a study of Shakespeare and T. S. Eliot, is best left to a computer. Always bent on following the latest trends, Dempsey promotes the methods of data mining and statistical analysis, which bypass the vagaries of traditional hermeneutics and textual interpretation altogether. By comparing the frequency of words and phrases found in both authors, Dempsey hoped to determine, quantitatively and precisely, once and for all, the influence the Bard had had on the Anglo-American modernist poet. "But my thesis isn't about that," McGarrigle demurs, frantically searching for a way to make this run-of-the-mill thesis in literary criticism sound more interesting and cutting-edge. He blurts out, much to his own surprise: "It's about the influence of T. S. Eliot on Shakespeare!"[1]

The audible gasp that goes through the room at this chronological impossibility was probably echoed by many of Lodge's readers in the 1980s, especially those who were not directly involved in that stormy academic decade that saw the rise of poststructuralism in British literary studies. McGarrigle continues to explain what he means, riffing and extemporizing, as he comes to realize that this spur-of-the-moment idea has legs:

> "Well, what I try to show," said Persse, "is that we can't avoid reading Shakespeare through the lens of T. S. Eliot's poetry. I mean, who can read Hamlet today without thinking of 'Prufrock'? Who can read the speeches of Ferdinand in *The Tempest* without being reminded of 'The Fire Sermon' section of *The Waste Land*?"[2]

Put this way, McGarrigle's proposal sounds rather sensible. It only seems shocking in a universe in which works of art are imagined to be under the exclusive control of the artists who created them. In this clarification, to be sure, McGarrigle's position has shifted somewhat: here it is no longer people influencing each other across centuries but influencing *our readings* of their works. This equivocation is based on the conviction that we never have unmediated access to the author's psyche and that any understanding of their work is always an interpretation, a projection that is filtered through our interests, cultures, and histories. What McGarrigle proposes is essentially a readerly aesthetic, in which literary works exist as texts, untrammeled by the precise conditions that brought them about in the first place, forever open to new readings and adaptable to new circumstances. Ultimately, in this text-based universe, authors become little more than figures that readers invoke in order to make sense of the sprawling network of relations between texts that could otherwise be drawn. From the perspective of reading, such texts can be related to one another irrespective of chronological precedence. A good half century after such seminal studies as Roland Barthes's "Death of the Author" (1967) and Michel Foucault's "What Is an Author?" (1969) came into circulation, these ideas need no longer shock and surprise us.[3] On the contrary, engagements with texts and artworks responding to each other—or rather, our allowing them to respond to each other, consciously reading one through the other—may enable us to gain a fresh perspective on those works.

It is with this gesture that I want to open this book on Beethoven's Ninth Symphony by considering it from the angle of a different-sounding artwork, the digital creation *9 Beet Stretch* (2002) by the Norwegian conceptual artist Leif Inge. This work exists on websites and apps and has been performed multiple times in various venues all over the world.[4] Put simply, Leif Inge took a CD recording of Beethoven's Ninth Symphony and "stretched" the duration of its sounds while preserving the pitch levels so that it lasted a whole twenty-four hours. In this book I aim to demonstrate, to borrow McGarrigle's flourish, Leif Inge's influence on Beethoven. (Maybe the starkness of this formulation, which seems to highlight the apparent absurdity of this claim, means that it has not lost all of its shock value after all.) Or, put more responsibly and somewhat provisionally, I will explore how our listening of Leif Inge's *9 Beet Stretch* can influence and potentially transform our experience of Beethoven's Ninth Symphony.

To be sure, the sounds we hear in Leif Inge's *9 Beet Stretch* bear at best very faint resemblance to Beethoven's symphony, and often none at all. (Excerpts can be heard on the accompanying website ▶.) The best way to make sense of the listening experience is probably to place it under the label of "ambient music." We hear amorphous sonic masses in the midst of slow and gradual change, which pass the ear at a glacial pace. The sounds we hear in *9 Beet Stretch* are curiously more dissonant than its faster counterpart; this is partly because the minuscule temporal differences from the individual players of the large symphony orchestra, as they change from one chord to the next, are blown up into gigantic proportions at such a slow speed, and partly because the smearing technique that is used in the granular synthesis underlying the technical process of slowing down the music augments such effects.

To savor McGarrigle's rhetorical pathos a little more, we should ask analogously about the consequences of such a listening experience: Who can listen to Beethoven's harmonies the same way once we have heard the grinding dissonances in Leif Inge's work? After experiencing the glacial slowness of *9 Beet Stretch*, is it still possible to approach the Ninth without a heightened awareness of its tempo modulations?

Lest we get hung up on questions of cultural status and aesthetic values too soon, we can and should expand this claim. I take Leif Inge's work, which we will examine

FIGURE 1.1   In 2016 Roger Baker mowed a gigantic head of Beethoven in his
lawn in the Catskills in New York. (Image: Piotr Redlinski/The
New York Times/Redux.)

in greater detail in chapters 3 and 4, more broadly as an illustration of how Beethoven is heard in the digital age. There is a certain irony in the fact that we have moved beyond McGarrigle's aversion to the interference of computer technology in matters of scholarly pursuit and have embraced it as a major driving force in this readerly aesthetics. Perhaps this is the difference between 1984, the year Lodge's *Small World* was published, and our own time; perhaps it is not necessary to think of the arts and information technology in oppositional terms. By now a sizeable body of literature, scholarly and popular, has given us ideas and a language to explore how the two sides can be brought together in productive ways, under the umbrella term of digital humanities.[5] Unlike Professor Dempsey's ideas about "big data," we are not taking the affordances of the digital realm here as a new tool for the analytical dissection of texts, a counting machine that can be discarded after its work is done. Instead, we will explore how the digital realm serves as a medium that allows us to encounter Beethoven's Ninth Symphony in fresh and new ways.[6]

BEETHOVEN'S NINTH IN THE DIGITAL AGE

The developments that became possible in the digital realm have transformed our engagement with the Ninth Symphony. These include not only radically different listening experiences such as 9 *Beet Stretch* but also, at the other extreme, a vastly accelerated version of the Ninth by Johannes Kreidler, a temporal contraction that only lasts a split second.[7] This "distillation" of Beethoven's symphony is part of Kreidler's *Compression Sound Art* (2009), a digital work by the enfant terrible of the German new music scene, in which the very definition of hearing gets stretched. Kreidler points out that it is just about possible to make out something resembling the human voice for a few milliseconds, right at the very end of the piece. This infinitesimal moment is the majestic choral finale of the Ninth. "Form becomes a detail," muses Kreidler.[8]

But beyond experiments with the sounding structure of the symphony, the digital revolution further reaches into a more rarefied realm concerning the score and performance history of the Ninth. Take the celebrated inscription of Beethoven's Ninth Symphony into the UNESCO Memory of the World register in 2001, as the first piece of music to be admitted to this collection of cultural heritage. Other than the intrinsic honor and responsibility that comes with this addition, the project has occasioned a digitization of the entire autograph score of the symphony. To musicians it may appear curious that the most prominent portion of this musical project focused on the score—that it to say, it remained in the visual domain—whereas the sounding aspect of the symphony seemed relatively irrelevant. Given the mission of the register, however—to "safeguard the documentary heritage of humanity against collective amnesia, neglect, the ravages of time and climatic conditions, and willful and deliberate destruction"—this emphasis on the autograph, the wellspring of all performances of the work, is perhaps understandable.[9] At the same time, it doubles as a telling commentary on the way in which the new millennium conceptualizes cultural memory, as inextricably coupled with archiving tasks, a point to which we will return in chapter 2. One side effect of this digitization project is that it highlights the fragmented existence of the autograph score. In its traditional material form, the manuscript is scattered between the Staatsbibliothek zu Berlin (which houses the lion's share of the autograph), the Bonn Beethovenhaus, and the Bibliothèque nationale de France in Paris. In the digital realm, this geographical dispersal fades into irrelevance—the autograph score exists complete in the virtual domain.[10]

Or take Stefan Weinzierl's virtual reconstructions of the acoustical space of the concert halls in which Beethoven's symphonies were premiered.[11] The building in which the Ninth first sounded, the Kärntnertortheater in Vienna, shown in figure 1.3, was torn down in 1870. But even though the material venue is lost, we can still catch an aural glimpse of the music that echoed through the hall on

FIGURE 1.2   The first page of the autograph of Beethoven's Ninth Symphony,
now digitized as part of the UNESCO Memory of the World
program. (Image: Stiftung Preussischer Kulturbesitz/bpk/artres.)

May 7, 1824. The computer algorithms that Weinzierl and
his team developed can recreate a highly nuanced sense of
the surprisingly short reverberation time that used to char-
acterize the acoustics of the famous Viennese stage.

Over the course of the next few chapters we will touch
on a range of further digital phenomena surrounding the
Ninth, including global synchronized performances and
flash mobs. Common to all these digital versions of the
Ninth is that they bring about experiences of the symphony
that would otherwise not be possible. In fact, the spectrum
of novel musical experiences opened up in this way is so
wide-ranging that it is tempting to speak of the Ninths in

FIGURE 1.3   The old Kärtnertortheater in Vienna, where Beethoven's Ninth
Symphony was first performed on May 7, 1824. (Image: Bildarchiv,
Österreichische Nationalbibliothek, E 22.390–D.)

the plural. Sometimes these digital versions of the Ninth
(re)create special experiential conditions; sometimes they
expand our notion of what hearing is. What links these dis-
parate instances of Beethoven's Ninth is that digital technology was used to transcend time and space. This is not
a coincidence, of course. In one way or another, the moti-
vation behind these diverse projects is invariably based on
the message of universal humanity that is so crucial to our
understanding of the symphony and that is at the same
time equally central to the promise of digital technology
overcoming vast spatial and temporal distances and creat-
ing what Marshall McLuhan called the "global village."[12]

Nor is it a coincidence that all these projects came about around the turn of the millennium. I will be thinking of the millennium and the dawn of the digital age as largely coterminous in this context, even though they obviously occupy very different cultural spheres.[13] The millennium is a moment in time—and, to be sure, a completely arbitrary one, which is nothing more than an accident of the way in which we count up time. Because of the heightened psychological significance of this numerical watershed, however, the millennium has attained a very real cultural significance. The digital age, by contrast, is best described as a watershed in technology. It started out with a novel way of processing data, but in its far-reaching ramifications modern digital technology has affected every aspect of our thinking. It would be difficult to claim a causal link between the millennium and digital technology, except perhaps in the technology-induced collective hysteria of the "Y2K" bug that briefly held the world captive in 1999 and that so neatly tied in with apocalyptic millennial visions in sacred and secular varieties. But the connection between the two is surely more than serendipitous—both convey, each in its own realm, a powerful sense of transition and transformation, of being on the threshold of something completely new.[14]

For our purposes, the new millennium seems to suggest—indeed, it demands—that we hear Beethoven's Ninth with different ears, in a way that allows us to explore the connections and the contrasts between "before" and "after the millennium." The means by which these new hearings of Beethoven's Ninth are achieved are based on digital technology.

CLEAN EARS FOR A NEW MILLENNIUM

The twenty-first century is a good time to clean out our ears. The later twentieth century was worried that the Ninth had suffered from continual overexposure. Critics lamented that, owing to its iconic status and unique cultural prestige, we hear the Ninth so much that we have forgotten how to listen to it. Cultural historian Michael Steinberg puts this concern well: "The more time we spend in the presence of [Beethoven's] music, the harder it is truly to hear it."[15] The innocent modifier "truly" does a lot of work here, but there is clearly a sense that Beethoven's Ninth is subjected to overuse, accumulating historical sediment, and that this has been to its detriment. A fresh disposition toward the work, it seems, must be uncovered—or perhaps rediscovered—by carefully reacquainting ourselves with the overly familiar symphony.

The ever-increasing volume with which Beethoven's Ninth was sounded in the run-up to the new millennium was broadly paralleled by a renewed interest in the thorny question of the meaning of the Ninth—though from a pointedly ambivalent angle that characterized what emerges in Nicholas Cook's rigorous historicization of the work as what might be called the "late-twentieth-century" Ninth.[16] Many of these efforts from the 1980s and '90s can be seen as attempts to dig deeper into the structure of the music to unearth some hidden subtleties and complexities, to listen more intently in order to pick up some of the undertones of the Ninth that may have eluded us in the din constantly surrounding us.

Maynard Solomon, for one, expressed confidence that Beethoven "quite consciously wanted us to find 'meaning' in the symphony,"[17] and urged his readers to listen more closely. He issued an invitation to hear the emergent shimmer of the open fifths that raise the curtain of the symphony as "an initial ambiguity leading to clarification."[18] Leo Treitler, too, cautioned his readers to attune their ears to the beginning of the symphony and to listen ever more closely. In his musically sensitive analysis, Treitler heard the symphony as beginning not with the first string sextuplets, as reproduced in example 1.1, but with the silence that precedes it, out of which ex nihilo the strings emerge.[19]

Treitler and Solomon heard a broad range of experiences in Beethoven's music, "touching upon such issues as creation, aggression, immensity, the ecstatic, the celestial, or if one were to attempt to find a single term to encompass them all, the transcendental."[20] But here Solomon avoided triumphant affirmation; instead he ended his analysis on a note of aporia. There is no certainty for Solomon, not even in Elysium. Fraternity merely "remains upon the horizon of possibility."[21] In these readings, the grammatical mood of the critical line "Alle Menschen werden Brüder" (All humans become brothers) effectively becomes the subjunctive. Similarly, Beethoven's heavenly father dwelling above the starry canopy—"Überm Sternenzelt muss ein lieber Vater wohnen"—is furnished with a "heart-rending question mark": he must still be sought in his abode beyond the stars. In this reading, the questioning *muss*, which gradually rises through the four vocal groups, suddenly sounds less like Friedrich Schiller and more like Bertolt Brecht, a century and a half later, in the haunting closing lines of his play *The Good Person of Szechuan* (1943). As Brecht's powerless gods disappear in a cloud, the helpless humans are left behind, and an actor implores the audience

EXAMPLE 1.1   Beethoven, Symphony no. 9, first movement, opening. Creatio
ex nihilo: the symphony begins with the silence before the
first notes.

EXAMPLE 1.1 Continued

in the epilog: "There must be a good [ending], must must must!" (Es muss ein guter da sein, muss, muss, muss!), as the curtain slowly drops.[22] The god that remains in the late-twentieth-century Ninth is a *deus absconditus*, an absent god. Cook takes up this thread and runs with it: at measures 650–54 of the finale, in example 1.2, he argues, at the unstable but insistent dominant ninth chords, "The music is the very embodiment of cosmic emptiness."[23]

If Solomon hears the ambiguous opening fifth as leading to eventual clarification, then the kind of clarity we finally reach is sobering. The only thing that reveals itself at the end of his subtle reading is that there is no way out of the initial ambiguity—the ambiguity Solomon hears is all-encompassing and total, reaching all the way down. The Ninth emerges enigmatically as a "symbol whose referents cannot be completely known and whose full effects will never be experienced."[24] Certainty is withheld; it is at best a distant glimmer of hope at the horizon. In the view that the late-twentieth-century Ninth projects, emptiness, doubt, and ambivalence prevail.

One commentator from those decades, Susan McClary, took a different—though similarly sobering—path, foregrounding the aspect of violence, specifically male sexual violence that she heard in the catastrophic return at the moment of recapitulation in the symphony's first movement. Generations of analysts have commented on this passage, in which the thematic material, in stark contrast to the mysteriously whispered and tonally ambiguous opening, returns in full force, in example 1.3, in an unstable but anything but tentative first-inversion D-major triad played fortissimo by the whole orchestra. Her analysis of

EXAMPLE 1.2   Beethoven, Symphony no. 9, fourth movement, mm. 650–54.
A questioning "Über Sternen muss er wohnen" seems to
indicate a *deus absconditus.*

EXAMPLE 1.3   Beethoven, Symphony no. 9, first movement, mm. 301–5.
The opening material returns with shocking force at the
beginning of the recapitulation.

EXAMPLE 1.3 Continued

EXAMPLE 1.3 Continued

this passage, celebrated and vilified in equal measure, drew particular attention to the explosive cadence that accompanies the failed homecoming, in a twisted harmonic progression, which she read in terms of male desire and frustration, pleasure and rage.[25] The response of the opposing camp, outraged by what was perceived as accusations of "Beethoven the Pornographer, Beethoven the Sexist," was swift and decisive.[26] (The lines between Beethoven the person and his work are similarly blurred in these criticisms, as in McGarrigle's project with which we started.) Critics charged that McClary's focus on sexuality, her embrace of politics, was one-dimensional, reductive, and overly specific.[27] As Robert Fink later clarified, the trope of violence, including sexual violence, was nothing new: it is, in fact, deeply embedded in the reception history of the Ninth, reaching back far into the nineteenth century. But in those days it had invariably been described from a male perspective. McClary's chief offense, it seems, boiled down to offering her feminist perspective on male violence.[28]

Though our trio of slightly earlier commentators, Cook, Treitler, and Solomon, did not take this controversy into account, their approaches are largely sympathetic to McClary's urge to push back against dominant narratives concerning the Ninth, except for one point: it was of paramount importance for the three that the Ninth be heard as a multivalent work that defies definitive pinning down. "For listeners today," Cook asserted, "the danger is of simply not hearing such things."[29] But we can ask further: If we cannot hope for a consolidated message at the bottom of these careful analyses, why do we listen to Beethoven's Ninth over and over again? "The critical task," Treitler explained, "is to interpret the text again (and again and again)." It is precisely the perpetual, open-ended act of interpretation, of meaning making, that is designed to shake us out of complacency and make us appreciate afresh the fundamental complexities and the unsettling weirdness that pervades much of the symphony.

The shared fear behind these bleak views of the Ninth is that of ideological appropriation, precisely of the kind that excessive consumption of the Ninth has fostered. The call to hear the cosmic nothingness of the Ninth, or, using Richard Taruskin's felicitous term, to continually "resist" the Ninth,[30] feeds into a broadly Adornian line of criticism. For the philosopher Theodor Adorno, modes of hearing the Ninth that gloss over ruptures, which would otherwise push listeners out of their comfort zones, were "affirmative"—such affirmation is to be resisted, in favor of grappling with the incongruities and gaps.[31] That is to say, the late-twentieth-century Ninth is not about nothing, but it is about the "big nothing"—the blind spots, the gaping holes torn in the order of knowledge and representation that perpetually haunt modernist art.[32]

The best way to resist appropriation of the Ninth—or so it seemed to these scholars writing at the close of the old millennium—is to prove that definitive meaning is not forthcoming. Such efforts to highlight elements of resistance, a resistance that is somehow immanent in the music and that can be uncovered with the tools of rigorous scholarship and careful interpretation, may assuage a scholarly world that is clearly uneasy with the affirmative and ideological message that the Ninth is habitually made to trumpet. This is a well-considered and wise position. But it also seems woefully ineffectual: the majority of musical listeners around the world seem completely oblivious to these concerns. Even serious music lovers among the Beethoven-consuming public seem nothing so much as bewildered by these discussions, which run counter to the obvious message that the symphony wears on its sleeve. The gap between the scholarly consensus and what concert audiences cherish most about the symphony could not be wider. The cost of recovering what it means to "truly hear" the Ninth is the yawning chasm between public message and scholarly interpretation, which lives on in splendid isolation.

If going deeper does not seem to have led us farther, then maybe it is time to take a different tack. It is tempting to suggest, after Karl Marx, that musicologists have merely interpreted the symphony—the point, however, is to change it.[33]

RE-HEARING THE NINTH

To be sure, the developments that Cook, Solomon, Treitler, and their colleagues observed with growing concern have only intensified on the other side of the millennium. To mention just one example, the newly re-established Iranian Orchestra in Tehran, which took up its business again in 2015 opening with—what else?—Beethoven's Ninth, made the startling announcement that it plans to perform the work every other week during its regular concerts.[34] There may well be practical reasons at play; after all, the orchestra has to build up a repertoire practically from scratch. But even from the perspective of a well-intentioned educator, this frequency would seem like overkill.

Now in its teenage years, the new millennium has clearly shown some distinctive traits. If the late-twentieth-century Ninth was all about a kind of all-or-nothing approach that vacillated between staring down the abyss and fighting ideological appropriation of the work, then the twenty-first-century Ninth is all about negotiating these two extremes. It is, quite literally, about bringing zeroes and ones together.

The digital medium allows a new kind of flexibility, and a renewed freedom that deliberately blurs the boundaries between re-creation and creation. Of course, this raises some important questions. Take the superhumanly slow version that the Ninth becomes in Leif Inge's hands or, for that matter, Kreidler's version, a blip that sounds more like a dial-up tone than like a symphony. Interesting though they are, can these things still be considered the Ninth? Though reasonable people may disagree, the answer I propose in chapter 3 is a resounding yes.

How does this digital art help us to (re-)learn to listen? Or, perhaps just as pertinently, how do we identify traces that allow us to analyze, understand, and recreate our listening practices? We can turn to at least two models here. First, an important theoretical impetus comes from the French philosopher Peter Szendy's book *Listen* (2001). Szendy urges us to take seriously the variety of versions in which music can exist: adaptations, arrangements, transcriptions, reworkings, orchestrations, paraphrases, fantasies, *réminiscences*, medleys, remixes—in a word, the debris of the musical work concept, particularly as it proliferated during the nineteenth century. Szendy encourages us to return once again to these cast-off versions, for they can be read, he argues, as historical documents that allow us a brief glimpse of nineteenth-century listening experiences. Arrangers, Szendy speculates, "may be the only listeners in the history of music that write down their listenings rather than describe them (as critics do)."[35] Each transcription requires certain editorial or compositional decisions, certain adaptations reflecting a particular listening perspective on the piece that is being transcribed.

The same is true of 9 Beet Stretch. We can think of this piece as a version of Beethoven's Ninth Symphony, made possible by computer technology. What makes Leif Inge's adaptation of this warhorse of the concert hall special is that it is not a re-hearing on paper, in the manner of a nineteenth-century piano arrangement, but it exists as a rendition—a special kind of performance, we might say—in the digital realm. 9 Beet Stretch bases its re-hearing on the sounds of a CD recording; that is, it manipulates digital code, not the notes of Beethoven's score. While this feature seems to make it categorically different from the kinds of nineteenth- and twentieth-century adaptations that Szendy had in mind, Leif Inge's piece can nonetheless shed light on listening habits, broadly construed, in the early twenty-first century. As we will explore in chapter 4, its digital code can be understood as a "written-down" version, even though it is legible not by human eyes but by a computer.

Our second model goes back to an idea proposed as early as 1977 by the French economist and musician Jacques Attali in his provocative study Noise, which can in this context be regarded as a radicalized version of Szendy's conception of the material traces of listening. In his book, Attali proposed a "political economy" of music proceeding through four stages.[36] With only a bit of oversimplification, these stages can be understood in terms of their predominant means of distribution or media: orality, printed notation, recordings, and a somewhat mysterious fourth stage, "composing." What Attali means by "composing" is different from what we normally think of as the activity of inventing and writing music. This "new way of making music" is perhaps best understood as a form of creative engagement on the basis of recorded music. In a world where music is perpetually available at our fingertips, Attali diagnoses, the act of collecting recordings—or "stockpiling" as he calls it—has lost its meaning. In this situation, he goes on to suggest, these recordings will become the material on which a new kind of creative practice is founded. From this perspective, the much-lamented condition of the Ninth, where we can no longer truly hear it because our world is so saturated with its sounds, would seem to be precisely the precondition of Attali's fourth stage.

Attali remained somewhat vague on the details.[37] Many commentators have interpreted "composing" as gesturing toward practices such as remixing, sampling, mash-ups, and other forms of electronic manipulation.[38] In the context of the digital age, where such techniques are relatively easy to accomplish, Attali's concept of "composition" muddies the traditional distinctions between composition (in its conventional sense) and performance, between author and consumer, and ultimately between past and future, in ways that have an immediate bearing on 9 *Beet Stretch*. It shifts the emphasis away from a stable work that demands to be interpreted and understood toward a messier, interactive engagement with musical material, which, in its existence as recorded sound, can now be accessed in wholly new manners, manipulated, reshaped, even recreated, in ways that were barely imaginable in previous times.

The ideas proposed by these two thinkers encourage us to pay attention to the media in which music is stored, processed, and reproduced. In both cases, media are not merely external features of the music, transparent carriers of sound that can be discarded or ignored, but an integral part of our story.[39] McLuhan's influential dictum "The medium is the message" is never far off.

This is where we can return to our adaptation of Marx: in Attali's fourth stage—which I will read here narrowly as essentially describing the affordances of the digital age— the listener is endowed with considerable powers to act creatively. In this light, the idea of changing the Ninth is not necessarily a clarion call for the revolution. Rather, it can be understood as an invitation to treat those creatively reimagined and altered versions with greater seriousness, as written-down listenings, in Szendy's sense, and to examine what these may tell us about the Ninth. This is where the idea of "written-down listenings" converges with Attali's "composition"[40]: both describe acts of inscription—that is, recording, processing, recalling—that blur the divisions between creation and recreation and that regard the medium as foundational to the act of listening.

00001001 (THE DIGITAL NINTH)

A skeptic might not be convinced by this. Is a digital work such as *9 Beet Stretch* even music? Isn't this just noise? *9 Beet Stretch*, for one, is based on an algorithm, on zeroes and ones, instead of notes in a score. This material distinction might sound appealing at first, but if we eliminate Leif Inge's piece on these grounds, we would also have to eliminate in one fell swoop all digitally recorded performances of the Ninth (which are also effectively nothing but zeroes and ones) and declare them non-music. We will have occasion over the course of the book to revisit this problem and its more philosophical implications. We will generally fare best if we make the case that *9 Beet Stretch* is epistemologically related to Beethoven's Ninth, even though ontologically they are distinct—that we know the two works to be abstractly related, even if they do not *sound* the same.

It is this double perspective, whether conceived as a Szendian "arrangement" or an Attalian "composition" of Beethoven's Ninth, that makes *9 Beet Stretch* such an interesting vantage point for our purposes. *9 Beet Stretch* is clearly a work of art that bears a close relationship to Beethoven's Ninth Symphony, but the specific listening perspective that it opens up allows us ways into the symphony to which we perhaps would not have been sensitive without Leif Inge's sound art. This is where we link back up with McGarrigle's ingenuity. Our task is made somewhat more straightforward than McGarrigle's reversal of Shakespeare and T. S. Eliot by the circumstance that Leif Inge's installation explicitly references Beethoven's Ninth Symphony and in fact bases itself on a CD recording of the symphony, whose digital code becomes its material. And certain aspects of the digital *9 Beet Stretch* focus our attention to specific characteristic features of the Ninth, including time, form, and noise.

Of course, there are certain consequences of this angle. To make headway in this brave new world, we have to retool a number of assumptions. As we have already seen, scores, performances, and even the musical work mean subtly but distinctly different things in this particular context. And, following McGarrigle, we will loosen the ties to Beethoven's authority and intention and will be paying attention instead to what the creation of Leif Inge's *9 Beet Stretch*, the details of its "score," its reception and aesthetics, can tell us about Beethoven's Ninth Symphony in the digital age. The context of other musical works in its orbit will be constituted less by nineteenth-century symphonic canonical works by composers who toiled in Beethoven's shadow and more by more recent creations by artists such as John Cage, Jem Finer, or Steve Reich.

The slow treatment that Beethoven's symphony undergoes in Leif Inge's hands, thanks to the technology of granular synthesis, places the Ninth far beyond the reaches of the symphonic canon, in close proximity to such icons of popular culture as Alfred Hitchcock's suspense movies and Justin Bieber's pop songs, both of which were subjected to similar processes of digital deceleration.[41] Does Beethoven's Ninth in our age, then, belong in the world of entertainment, the world of horror special effects and pop music? As a question of aesthetic value, there is no simple answer. But as a cultural question, it is true that Beethoven's Ninth, like few other works from the classical canon, occupies an enormous place in the popular imagination that rivals mass-cultural phenomena, including movies and pop music. For a broader answer, we should expand the cultural circle further. After all, an interest in slowness is nothing new. The "slow movement" gained traction starting in the 1980s as a critique of the fast-lived and ever-accelerating culture we live in, a protest against the relentless pace of modern life: slow food, slow money, slow cities, slow movies, slow living.[42] In this context, Leif Inge's decelerated version can be understood as a commentary on modern mass culture, with all that entails.

Despite the emphasis on newness that is an almost inescapable part of any discussion of digital culture, the musical questions surrounding slowness and its concomitant features—scale and format, time and form, history and monumentality, incomprehensibility and the sublime—did not, of course, suddenly emerge out of thin air; they have a long history that stretches back into Beethoven's nineteenth century and far beyond. Our exploration of the Ninth with its focus on developments in the digital realm will go beyond the particulars of digital art and open up the view to features of Beethoven's symphony in other (more conventional) guises. It is in this sense that we should understand, for now, my invocation of McGarrigle's anti-chronological position vis-à-vis the influence of Leif Inge on Beethoven.

When we had our imaginary skeptic ask rhetorically "Is *9 Beet Stretch* not just noise?" the answer is clearly yes: it is noise. But it is a special kind of noise. Indeed, the very question about "noise" gains new significance in the context of digitization. We are talking about data streams, with their "signal-to-noise ratios," which determine our situation to a greater extent than we are often willing to admit. The creative expression communicated by the symphony in the digital realm may be different from what we are used to, and this may require some adjustments. Musical forms, traditionally regarded as the principal conveyor of symphonic meaning, don't necessarily carry a lot of weight when they are reduced to a feature in the digital realm, once temporal relations get squishy. But this does not imply that they carry no meaning. On the contrary, once we renegotiate this new territory, a fairly coherent cluster of ideas becomes discernible in these sounds from the virtual realm, its global community and the instant access, its redefinition of time and space, that allows us to rethink the very meaning of this music from the ground up. If the conclusions we reach can be generalized beyond their immediate impact on the Ninth Symphony, then this is a desired side effect. In the final analysis, the Digital Ninth, the Millennial Ninth, is centrally concerned with temporality, with the experience of time. This is the reason this book gives pride of place to this slowed-down version. It's about time.

CHAPTER 2

MARKING HISTORY

I N 1989 TIME SEEMED to stand still. On November 9 the Berlin Wall crumbled. The Cold War was declared over. The "short" twentieth century drew to a close.[1] During that year, the neoliberal scholar Francis Fukuyama triumphantly proclaimed no less than "the end of history."[2] Reviving Hegelian universal history, Fukuyama argued that history was inexorably moving in one direction. Driven by the joined forces of capitalism, science, and liberal democracy, the goal of history, he explained, was the attainment of freedom.[3] And with the end of the Cold War, Fukuyama continued with panache, that process was completed. History itself had ground to a halt.

This does not mean that the world comes to an end. After the end of history, the argument goes, things can still happen. It's just that no event has any relevance for the process that history was destined to accomplish. In this model, for Hegel as well as for Fukuyama, opposing forces were dismissed as mere distractions that did not possess any actual "reality," as Hegel would have put it, because they lacked viability and were ultimately irrelevant. Such blips on the radar included Islamic fundamentalism, the Chinese economy, and the green movement—that is to say, forces that have in retrospect turned out to be quite a bit bigger than they may have appeared from Fukuyama's vantage point of 1989.[4]

With the benefit of hindsight, it seems that this period was at most a plateau, a "holiday from history,"[5] as a prominent conservative commentator put it, which was sharply curtailed by the events of September 11, 2001. But in the euphoria of the 1990s, in the dozen years between 11/9 and 9/11, when many in the West believed they had won a decisive victory in the Cold War, those pesky issues may well have seemed inconsequential—or devoid of Hegelian reality.

BERNSTEIN'S NINTH, BEETHOVEN'S SCHILLER

Around the same time a renewed interest in Beethoven's Ninth Symphony was noticeable. Of course, this warhorse of the concert hall had never gone out of style. But distinctive ways in which the work was approached and distinctive ends to which it was put emerged during those years. A number of self-consciously historic performances of the work were staged that transcended the concert hall and took on a life of their own. In a world where the end of history had been decreed, it seems, it became all the more important to mark events as historic by other means. Beethoven's Ninth served as the perfect vehicle to convey the importance and solemnity of those moments to worldwide audiences.

It is fitting to start with media star Leonard Bernstein's much-noted and symbol-laden performance of December 1989. Under Bernstein's baton, Beethoven's symphony was performed over the Christmas holiday on both sides of the newly toppled Berlin Wall with an international ensemble of instrumentalists and singers. For anyone who was still not sufficiently sensitized to the heightened historic significance of this performance, Bernstein made a change to Schiller's poem, inserting the word "freedom" (Freiheit) wherever Beethoven's score required "joy" (Freude).[6] The world took notice of this replacement. In our age textual changes have become a rare event and therefore always attract attention. There is no doubt that Bernstein's decision was grounded in his idealism and his genuine enthusiasm for the historical moment. This, he explained, was "a heaven-sent moment to sing *'Freiheit'* wherever the score indicates the word *'Freude.'* "[7] But he still felt the need to justify his decision in terms that would go beyond his personal beliefs, to somehow ground it in Beethoven's intentions.

As Bernstein conceded in his explanatory note, the change is academically unsound, since there is no documentation of Beethoven's intentions for this part of the score. But he pointed to a long (and entirely spurious) tradition—a "conjecture,"[8] as Bernstein put it delicately—of thinking about "joy" as a code word for "freedom" in the context of Schiller's ode, since explicit mention of freedom

FIGURE 2.1   The neoclassical Konzerthaus in former East Berlin, where
Bernstein conducted his "Ode to Freedom" in 1989, is adorned by
a statue or Friedrich Schiller, the poet of "An die Freude."

would, apparently, not have passed the strictures of censorship of the time. This conjecture can be traced back to the 1830s, just a few years after Beethoven's death. It started its life in an inauspicious place, in a piece of fiction, in a footnote, no less, from the novella *Das Musikfest oder die Beethovener* (1838) by Wolfgang Griepenkerl.[9] From there it took many different guises—from contrafactum and biographical reflection via rumor and denial all the way to repeated academic assertion.[10] Bernstein's change to the text, though a drastic measure by anyone's standards, was only the latest instance in this long reception history. There is no factual historical basis for his claim, but it is striking that the idea of the Ninth encoding freedom flares up again and again in every generation. Whatever else can be said about it, there is clearly a long-lived cultural desire for this story to be true.

The apocryphal story of a clandestine "Ode to Freedom," as an attempt to preempt censorship, is helped by two factors. First, Schiller did make some significant changes to the poem when he revised it in 1803 with the view to including it in an anthology, published some twenty-one years before Beethoven completed his score. Schiller included the poem mostly on account of its already notable popularity, but he expressed unhappiness with the youthful and enthusiastic tone of the original poem (1786) and felt that it needed to be reworked. It was precisely those verses that espoused the values of the French Revolution most clearly—*liberté, égalité, fraternité*—that were muted or cut in the revisions. The important line "All men become brothers" (Alle Menschen werden Brüder) was originally the more radical "Beggars become the brothers of princes" (Bettler werden Fürstenbrüder). And the stanza that included the rallying cry for "rescue from tyrants' chains" (Rettung von Tyrannenketten) was omitted altogether in the final version.[11]

Here we should pause to ask: If freedom was indeed too sensitive to be mentioned explicitly in 1824, when Beethoven set these radical lines, then how had they made it past the censor in the first place? The severity of censorship changed over time—in Vienna, Schiller's stage plays were censored between 1793 and 1808, after which time they were very popular in Viennese theatres.[12] Concerns about censorship were running particularly high during Metternich's chancellorship (1821–1848)—that is, the period during which the myth first flared up—with its severe state apparatus and its heavy-handed practice of censorship, more so than the early 1780s, when Schiller first penned "An die Freude," or the early 1800s, when Schiller resided in Weimar as a celebrated poet. Literary scholars generally agree that Schiller's revisions are less the result of censorship and more an act of self-censorship. As is well known, Schiller become more and more disillusioned with the way in which the French Revolution developed, and his editorial changes reflect the way he moderated his initial fervent support over time.[13] In the revised version, the ideals of the revolution came effectively under erasure.

Details of Beethoven's setting of the poem reveal that he was familiar with both versions of Schiller's text. Tellingly, he chose to include one verse from the original version, preferring the more urgent "Laufet, Brüder, eure Bahn" (Run, brothers, your course) over of the later version with its more stately pace, "Wandelt, Brüder" (Walk, brothers).[14] But for the most part he followed Schiller's revisions, which may be less ardent in their support of revolutionary ideals, but which also propound a stronger sense of universalism.

Moreover, as Gail K. Hart reminds us, our collective memory is far more attuned to Beethoven's version of the "Ode to Joy" than to Schiller's original poem (in either version).[15] It was Beethoven's editorial red pen that by and large determined our reception of Schiller's text. In fact, Beethoven's extensive cuts and reorderings turned Schiller's verses into a more compressed and elevated ode by significantly altering the structure of the poem.[16]

Schiller's original has been identified as a *geselliges Lied*, a "convivial song," or, put more directly, a drinking song. There is a light-hearted, even raucous side to the poem that Beethoven largely eliminated from his version and that we consequently tend to overlook. This seems to balance the explicit passages on suffering that Beethoven also excised from his version of the poem. Schiller's original poem winds up, in a distinctly over-the-top mood, with toasts and good wishes for everybody—including gentleness for cannibals ("trinken Sanftmut Kannibalen") and a long life even for the dead ("Auch die Toten sollen leben!"). These sentiments are not taken up in Beethoven's ode—the rousing cheers would fit only awkwardly within the more homogeneously elevated style that prevails in Beethoven's selections. Only rudiments of this ebullient side remain, such as the ribald and alliterative image of the lowly, lustful worm ("Wollust ward dem Wurm gegeben"), which in Beethoven's version is all too easily passed over in favor of the sublime cherub standing before God.[17] Gone is the wine splashing heavenward and, with it, the more physical and exuberant Bacchic ideal of joy that speaks out of Schiller's verses.[18]

The images of joy that are preserved in Beethoven's version transform, distill, and channel the intoxication of Schiller's song into a clearer spiritual affinity to some notion of freedom. No wonder that Bernstein's intervention into the sung text works without problems. He would have had a much harder time switching *Freude* for *Freiheit* in the boozier parts of Schiller's poem. It is tempting to call Beethoven's revisions a more sober affair as compared with Schiller's versions, but this would be misleading: Schiller's enthusiastic tone is clearly retained in Beethoven's version too.[19] What Beethoven's changes to Schiller's poem present, rather, is a version that could be more readily understood as a code to be cracked by posterity. The "Ode to Joy" that we know was ultimately Beethoven's work. But in light of Schiller's reputation as the "poet of freedom," what Beethoven had done more specifically—and Bernstein in his wake—was to make Schiller's poem more Schillerian.

MEMORY AND HISTORY

Bernstein's performance, whose significance as a musical interpretation is by far eclipsed by its iconic cultural status, was in every sense a turning point. Let's pause here for a brief methodological reflection. We started with Bernstein's curiously contorted argument in support of his change, for which he invoked a historical precedent in nineteenth-century thought, even though he suspected it was a sham. Bernstein's performance amounts to a restaging of a nineteenth-century myth that had passed gradually from the realm of fiction to that of rumor and finally to culturally sanctioned truth.

We can best make sense of Bernstein's quandary from the perspective of the terms history and memory. These paired terms are key to a better understanding of the position of the Ninth in our culture. The French historian Pierre Nora has developed the concept of the *lieux de mémoire*, often translated as "realms of memory," which plays an important role here. These *lieux*—places—are not necessarily physical places or sites.[20] They can also include moveable or immaterial objects, cultural products, even abstract concepts, as long as they serve to trigger collective memories. Nora sets up his concept of the memory site in a strictly national (French) context, and other national schools of historians have followed him in identifying similar sites. In a comparable project focusing on German collective memory, Beethoven's Ninth is in fact included as a "memory site," or *Erinnerungsort*—the only such site based on a work of classical music.[21]

Nora's notion is, at bottom, indebted to an organic notion of memory—messy, imprecise, imaginative—which borders on the romantic, with all that entails. His opening salvo sets up his program in explicitly nostalgic terms: "We speak so much of memory because there is so little of it left."[22] Nora posits a past Golden Age—before writing, before modernity, something of a pastoral idyll—in which memory flowed freely and formed a living connection between past and present. Modern life, he argues, has encroached on this *milieu de mémoire* so that what was once a flowering, all-embracing memoryscape only remains in a few isolated *lieux*. Like nature reserve areas, Nora asserts, these rare *lieux* must be protected at all costs. The *lieux de mémoire* are contrasted with the more rigorous and bureaucratic domain of history, by which Nora specifically means archival and documentary history.[23] At bottom, however, Nora is convinced that there is a fundamental truth to memory, which eludes even the most precise historical documentation; memory allows us to connect experientially to the past. Such a shared memory establishes a sense of group identity that can be projected onto the present and into the future.

Nora decries the decline of memory as it turns more and more into "sifted and sorted historical traces." This modern, archival form of memory has all but replaced the "integrated, dictatorial memory," which Nora relishes describing as "unself-conscious, commanding, all-powerful, spontaneously actualizing, a memory without a past that ceaselessly reinvents tradition, linking the history of its ancestors to the undifferentiated time of heroes, origins, and myth." In our modern age, Nora adds wistfully, memory is separated by an unbridgeable gulf from history: "What we call memory today is therefore not memory but already history." The conflict between memory and history suggests a distinction between (felt) authenticity and (documentary) correctness—between hearts and minds, as it were.[24]

A lot of what Nora describes plays out in the historically charged soundings of Beethoven's Ninth—down to the conflict between history and memory in contemporary culture. Bernstein's "Ode to Freedom" clearly appeals to the emotional depth of the moment, which would surely be sufficient to justify the change (even if not everybody might agree with it). Yet Bernstein still felt the need to legitimate his decision with references to historical documentation—even if this documentation, literally based in fiction, is known to be false. The veracity of the historical documentation seemed to be less important than the much more basic fact that there was documentation available.

OFFICIAL PERFORMANCES

Bernstein's Ninth at the Berlin Wall garnered much media attention and set the scene for the wholehearted embrace of the Ninth as a *lieu de mémoire*. A diverse range of official and ceremonial media spectacles, each very different from the others, followed in its wake over the next few years. One such outstanding occasion for the Ninth was the Olympic Games in 1998.

It is not widely known that several of the most spectacular traditions surrounding the Olympic Games originated with Hitler's notorious 1936 games in Berlin. The lighting of the Olympic fire and the ceremonial passing of the torch from Greece to the place at which the games are held, for instance, is not an archaic rite but an invention of Goebbels's Ministry for Propaganda. Another such tradition is the performance of Beethoven's Ninth during Olympic ceremonies.[25] The founder of the modern Olympic movement, Pierre de Coubertin, had long hoped that Beethoven's music would be incorporated in the ceremonies, as he felt the choral symphony resonated with the spirit of the Olympic Games. So the aging Coubertin was especially delighted to note that the 1936 games in Berlin incorporated the symphony in their opening ceremony—in an adaptation, to be sure, accompanying grandiose pageantry that was widely admired by the international spectators. Subsequent games, starting with Mexico City in 1968, have often incorporated the "Ode to Joy" in their closing ceremonies.

The Winter Games of 1998 in Nagano took this tradition one important step further. Under the baton of Seiji Ozawa, director of the Boston Symphony Orchestra and the most prominent international conductor of Japanese origin, a global performance of the Ninth took place on five continents simultaneously. While a chorus of two thousand and eight international soloists sang in situ, these singers were joined by choruses and orchestras performing the work in Beijing, Berlin, Cape Town, New York, and Sydney. The real feat of this performance was the precise synchronization of music from around the globe, thanks to digital technology that improved the critical time lag of satellite transmission. The full effect of this global performance of the work only unfolded on the screens at the Minami Stadium and on TVs all over the world.[26]

It is no coincidence that this massed Olympic performance of Beethoven's Ninth took place in Japan. There *daiku* (or "big nine") is a long-standing popular tradition, usually carried out at the end of the year, where large amateur choruses, which can encompass thousands of singers, perform the Ninth. Its status is perhaps comparable with Handel's Messiah in the English-speaking world, though its dimensions and cultural impact are possibly greater.[27] Ozawa was actively encouraging audience participation through TV screens worldwide. Even viewers just humming along at home, he urged, should join in: "People all over the world singing together about joy—that's the purpose."[28] Ozawa's Olympic Ninth was a global *daiku*, with an imagined community worldwide brought together by collective singing, from the comfort of one's home.

Two years later, the Ninth was put to very different ends. In 2000, the British conductor Simon Rattle directed the work with the Vienna Philharmonic Orchestra at the site of the former Mauthausen concentration camp to commemorate the fifty-fifth anniversary of its liberation. The choice of the Ninth for this occasion, and this location, raised several eyebrows.[29] Originally Mahler's *Resurrection* Symphony had been favored, under the direction of Zubin Mehta.[30] But the Ninth won the day. Even before it happened, scandal was brewing. The controversial performance was destined to become either a "most ennobling" or "most ill-conceived"[31] event—either way, it would be an occasion to remember.

Significantly, Rattle thought of the performance not as an event so much as a ritual.[32] In Mauthausen, the Ninth was bookended by Jewish prayers, preceded by a musical arrangement of El Male Rachamim, a funeral prayer that is at times invoked in the context of the Holocaust, and followed by a recitation of Kaddish, the ritual praise of God in the face of mourning. Instead of applause following the performance of the Ninth, the audience was instructed to silently light a candle. The jury was out on this controversial performance: Was it a moving tribute, even something approaching a ritual cleansing from the Nazi atrocities that had taken place in the concentration camp, on the very soil where the sounds of Beethoven's "Ode to Joy" were now reverberating? Or was it a tasteless media spectacle in which listeners were reduced to the status of mass ornaments? Loud voices on both sides made themselves heard.

In this context, it is hard not to think of the line from the "Ode to Joy," "Your magic reconnects that which custom had strictly divided" (Deine Zauber binden wieder, was die Mode streng geteilt), in which reconciliation and reuniting occupy central positions, as a central message. In this extreme context, such sentiments may seem at best naïve, heartfelt though they may have been. Indeed, the danger of focusing on one textual passage and applying it to a specific historical situation is highlighted in the immediate continuation of the ode, when the second verse begins:

Freude trinken alle Wesen
an dem Busen der Natur
alle guten, alle bösen
folgen deiner Rosenspur.

All creatures drink joy
At the bosom of nature
All good ones, all evil ones
Follow your rosy trail.

In this situation of moral extremes, against a background of the Holocaust as the representation (or indeed the non-representation) of absolute evil, can such sentiments be even remotely appropriate? "Joy is rather indiscriminate in what it brings together,"[33] philosopher James Schmidt concluded wryly, in the face of the profound moral ambivalence of this televised ritual.

And finally, as if to punctuate the end of the "end of history" myth by musical means, the American conductor Leonard Slatkin was faced with the delicate issue of having to conduct the Last Night of the Proms in London, which was scheduled for September 15, 2001, only a few days after four hijacked planes crashed into New York's World Trade Center, the Pentagon, and a field in rural Pennsylvania. The Proms, or Promenade Concerts, are a major classical music event during the summer season in London, and the Last Night especially is something of a celebration of Britishness. In light of the tragic events, the scheduled program—with its traditional patriotic favorites and John Adams's *Short Ride in a Fast Machine*, of all things—seemed grossly inappropriate. The jolly patriotic outfits and Union Jacks that are usually donned on this occasion also stayed at home that year. The substitute program featured Adams's *Tromba lontana*, Barber's *Adagio for Strings*, a selection of spirituals from the oratorio *A Child of Our Time* by the British composer Michael Tippett (carefully omitting the

movement "Go Down, Moses"), as well as the last movement of Beethoven's Ninth Symphony. The "Ode to Joy"
here defiantly countered the tragedy and the shock of 9/11.
The concert concluded with a rousing rendition of Hubert
Parry's anthem "Jerusalem" as a nod to the traditional program that many in the audiences had expected. It was suggested at the time, bizarrely, that Beethoven's *Missa solemnis*
would have been more apt—possibly in light of the dedica-
tion: "From the heart, may it go back to the hearts."[34] But
the explicitly religious dimension of the terrorist attack
would have made this work with its place in the Christian
liturgy problematic.

There are few specific connecting points among these
occasions that call for mourning or rejoicing. As the
Mauthausen performance makes particularly clear, the
function of Beethoven's symphony is not dissimilar from
that of a liturgical work, but it operates within the flexibility of a secular context. Triumph, togetherness, sorrow,
defiance—the Ninth has it all. Freed from the explicitly religious function of a Te Deum or a Requiem in the
Christian tradition, the symphony served in all these performances to punctuate history, highlighting for us the
things that matter, that are declared historic, and charg-
ing those things emotionally, at a time when history had
apparently ended.

What do we do with a situation in which Beethoven's
Ninth plays with history? A situation in which the general
meaningfulness of the Ninth supplants the precise meaning of the work? A situation that toys with the aura of his-
toricity, or rather with a pointedly experiential kind of
history? These concerns lead us further into the realm of

memory, sharing much with history, as it does, but following its own logic.

The very act of sounding Beethoven's Ninth at the Berlin Wall, at the Olympics, at Mauthausen, and after 9/11 guides collective remembrance. And in all these cases, the audiences by far exceeded the groups of people assembled in the auditorium: media participation, the broadcasting of these performances to audiences all over the world, was an essential part of these concerts. Or, in Schiller's words: "Seid umschlungen, Millionen, diesen Kuss der ganzen Welt" (Be embraced, ye millions, / This kiss goes out to the whole world). These performances self-consciously addressed themselves to a global viewership—at least to that part of the world that Fukuyama had in mind when he proclaimed the end of history.

PROTEST PERFORMANCES

Even at the time, not everybody agreed that history had in fact ended. Outside the West, the world looked very different. And in parallel, a different political performance history of Beethoven's Ninth is discernible. There, in various parts of the world, we observe a tendency to take the Ninth out of the concert halls—literally in this case, not just figuratively—and to bring it directly into the streets.

In 1989, during the Chinese student uprising, amplified recordings of Beethoven's Ninth Symphony were prominently used by the protesters to drown out the political speeches and proclamations of the Party, as seen in the video 2.1 ⏵.[35] The choice of Beethoven's Ninth is not coincidental. Not only does it carry the political overtones of which others also partook, but it also played a heightened role during the Cultural Revolution in China in the 1960s, which was becoming relevant again a generation later, in a movement that was branded as counterrevolutionary by officials and that tragically culminated in the Tiananmen massacre on June 4, 1989.

During that earlier period in the 1960s, Chinese politicians and intellectuals had debated whether Beethoven's symphony was Western, bourgeois, capitalist, or even totalitarian.[36] From the perspective of Maoist orthodoxy, the symphony was criticized for yielding to the "illusion of progress without conflict" toward a just society and for muddling one's "class viewpoint for understanding problems."[37] Others had held, by contrast, that the spirit of humanism in the ode transcended prevailing feudalism, and that the symphony should therefore be seen as an ally of the proletariat. The joy expressed in Beethoven's music, the argument continued, should be understood as a "victory through struggle," a concept that can be fitted without problems into a Marxist-Maoist ideology.[38] All of these past discussions resonated in the use of the symphony by the Chinese students in 1989. It is difficult not to think of the cry "Alle Menschen" in this context—and no less so than in light of the worldwide criticisms of China's human rights violations that followed in the wake of the massacre.

At the other end of the world, in Chile during the Pinochet dictatorship (1973–90), many women, demanding to know the whereabouts of their disappeared husbands, fathers, and sons—the so-called *desaparecidos*—would hold up signs in peaceful protest showing pictures of their missing loved ones. As described in video 2.2 ▶, the women would break their silence to chant the *himno de la alegría*, the "Hymn of Joy," outside of the prisons where many of the political opponents were held. Those prisoners who survived relate that they could hear the singing and knew that they had not been forgotten.[39]

It is not wrong to call the *himno de la alegría* a protest song. The Spanish version, in the popular arrangement by the Argentine composer Waldo de los Ríos, was self-consciously conceived as a Hispanic "We Shall Overcome," the protest song of the American civil rights struggle in the 1960s.[40] The arrangement plays with the sound of the symphony orchestra and highlights from Beethoven's score but also assigns prominent roles to folk guitar strumming and elements from easy listening traditions, including a rhythm group and a violin descant. The Chilean writer Ariel Dorfman reminisces on this time: "Why were we singing? To give ourselves courage, of course, but not only that. In Chile, we sang and stood against the hoses and tear gas and truncheons, because we knew that somebody else was watching."[41] This "somebody else" included not only the prisoners and their guards but, more widely, the world watching on TV screens worldwide. There was every reason to believe that the choice of the "Ode to Joy," as an expression of the hope that one day all humans might indeed come together in brotherhood, would be understood in all corners of the world.

Other protest movements have availed themselves of the "Ode to Joy" as a universal song of protest or of celebration, including the Germans in 1989 who wasted no time and climbed up onto the Berlin Wall soon after the border checkpoints were opened and hundreds of East Berliners streamed westward. From there, perched on top of the wall, the occupiers sang (among other things, to be sure) the "Ode to Joy," as a grassroots counterpoint to the official performances that were to follow in the East Berlin Konzerthaus only a few weeks later under the baton of Leonard Bernstein.[42] And, in true grassroots fashion, these renditions were typically accompanied not by a symphony orchestra but by impromptu guitars.

All of these protesters throughout the world could hear the ongoing march of history quite clearly, and it followed the rolling trochees of Beethoven's ode. Unlike the polished official celebratory and commemorative performances in the West, played by professional orchestras and staged as media events, these unkempt communal renditions of the Ninth—or, more often than not, the "Ode to Joy" as the

FIGURE 2.2   Singing Germans on the Berlin Wall in 1989. (Image: dpa.)

distillation of the symphony—all took an active part in the political events surrounding them. The chanting protesters in these popular movements had different goals; the movements arose out of different political situations; and they used Beethoven's Ninth to a range of different ends. But common to all was that Beethoven's music gave them something to hold on to; as they reported over and over again, it gave them hope.[43] Bernstein's *Freiheit*—which gave expression to the explosive political power of the Ninth by explicitly inscribing it into the fabric of the symphony—was, they firmly believed, not far off.

The Ninth is now a global phenomenon. Or rather, as Lewis Lockwood has observed, the Ninth is actually two phenomena.[44] On the one hand it's the "brilliant, glossy, 'official' performance,"[45] in Rose Rosengard Subotnik's description, and on the other hand the grassroots renditions that turn the Ninth into something closer to a protest song, focusing pars pro toto on the "Ode to Joy." For all the important differences between them, the "gloss" and "grassroots" performances are unified in at least one point: Beethoven's Ninth—like few other pieces of Western music—articulates history. Its significance is crystal clear; in fact, it is *all too* clear. But its specific meaning, as we have seen, is less important than the aura of meaningfulness in which is it is cloaked. For better or worse, Beethoven's Ninth has become the soundtrack of our time.

THE GLOBAL NINTH

Perhaps, though, the gloss / grassroots divide, which essentially replicates the high art / low art divide, is doing us a disservice. And, it seems, over the last few years a new mode of presenting Beethoven's Ninth has taken up elements of both—the Beethoven Nine flash mob. This is a prime example of the (re-)creative activity that characterizes Attali's stage of "composition." While the flash mob is now a phenomenon that is closely associated with the internet, specifically with documentation on YouTube, it is useful to remember that the idea of the flash mob precedes the popular video platform. First reported in 2003, the flash mob is both subversive and often uplifting: a group of people suddenly assemble in a public space and take it over for an apparently spontaneous act, after which they disperse again.[46] Social critique may be an object of flash mobs, but more often than not they fall under the category of random acts of kindness and senseless acts of beauty. There is always something vaguely unsettling about flash mobs, in that they invariably begin out of what we assume to be an anonymous mass of people, only to turn out in fact to be carefully coordinated, choreographed, and rehearsed. All flash mobs suggest that things are not what they appear to be, and they serve as reminders that the general public is subject to scrutiny and control at all times.[47] However, because of their usually benign content, it can also be argued that flash mobs remind us how even in a world of near-total control, subversive acts, events out of the ordinary, are possible. No doubt because of their fleeting existence, it seems almost inevitable that flash mobs will be captured and distributed on the internet. If it's not on YouTube, as they say, it didn't happen.

It should not be too surprising that by far the most popular version of Beethoven's Ninth on YouTube is a flash mob, viewed some 73 million times.[48] (The fact that the video went viral probably owes a lot to the fact that the famous neurologist and writer Oliver Sacks, as he lay dying in 2015, linked to it in his final tweet, calling it a "beautiful way to perform one of the world's great musical treasures.")[49] It is not without irony, in this genuinely heartfelt comment, that this flash mob was organized as a promotion by a Catalan bank, Banc Sabadell.

There are so many other flash mobs of Beethoven's Ninth available on YouTube that a case can be made that by now there exists a standard flash mob format for the work, outlined in example 2.2. This has a lot to do with the idealized choreography of the flash mob, the gradual emergence of participants out of the indistinct mass, which corresponds well with the variation form in which Beethoven presents the "Ode to Joy" in the last movement. A single instrumentalist, a double bass player, stands in a public place busking. The performance is prompted by a passerby engaging with the musician. The "Joy" theme begins unaccompanied, at m. 92, and here the busker is often joined by a cellist. Gradually more musicians emerge on the scene and play along. While the Sabadell performance follows Beethoven's instrumentation—lower strings and bassoon—it simplifies the score, playing only a very rudimentary bassline (with at times awkward voice leading), as shown in example 2.1. Most flash mobs have such a simplified bassline; the original contrapuntal version from Beethoven's score is rarely heard. This may have practical reasons: in a public space, before the conductor has made an appearance, Beethoven's complex and archaic contrapuntal texture is fairly difficult to coordinate.[50] As the flash mob performance continues,

EXAMPLE 2.1   (a) The contrapuntal version in which Beethoven presents his
theme, starting at m. 112, has posed a challenge in flash mob
versions of the Ninth. (b) The texture is greatly simplified
in the version preferred in most flash mobs, substituting a
simple harmonic bass line.

(a)

(b)

more strings emerge gradually, and eventually the conductor steps forward to present the same simplified version,
with subtly doubled thirds. A tutti breaks forth, largely
modeled on the orchestral version from mm. 178–187 of

EXAMPLE 2.2   A diagrammatic version of the strophic form that has become
the standard for flash mobs of the Ninth. The Catalan text
used in the Sabadell version follows the translation by Joan
Maragall.

BEETHOVEN'S SYMPHONY NO. 9

EXAMPLE 2.2   Continued

Beethoven's score, but here with choral parts added. The performance then cuts straight to the retransition at the end of the fugue, m. 521, with the dotted horn rhythms presenting a kind of intermediary fanfare. The tutti chorus returns, now against the triplet accompaniment of mm. 543–590, before cutting to the final prestissimo at m. 920. This is definitely a "highlights" version of the piece, an arrangement that flattens out the formal complexities of the movement in favor of a fairly simple strophic design, with a steady progression of increasingly larger forces, and increasingly fast rhythms. But it also speaks to a format that feels comfortable to the typical listening situation of our age, characterized as it is, for better or for worse, by a near-permanent state of distractedness. Six minutes seems about the maximum length that a music video is capable of holding our attention.

There is a curious ambiguity in the fact that Banc Sabadell's flash mob, which sets its choreography in the reassuring quietude of a small-town square in Spain, has all the trappings of a commercial enterprise. Its production values are immaculate, and its advertising aspects are subtly underplayed. A child drops a coin in the hat in front of the lone musician in the square, whose musical improvisation seems to allude to the Beatles' "With a Little Help from My Friends," before it launches into the "Ode to Joy." The flash mob takes place in front of the main office of the bank on the square, but the façade only makes a passing and understated appearance. Much time is spent showing close-ups of the enraptured faces of the listening crowd. No wonder that many viewers at home were deceived, as the comments section suggests, into believing that the spontaneity of the whole event was real—against the odds, despite the professional photography and the masterful editing.

Flash mobs such as this one occupy a strange middle ground between authentic and staged events. The performance of the symphony, and the recording of it, were clearly choreographed and planned, but they may well have remained a surprise to some of the passersby. For a brief period of time, about six minutes, the spectators are removed from their everyday activities; the magical concert out of nowhere imposes a moratorium on mundaneness. This mix of knowing and unknowing plays with boundaries between reality and fiction and is perhaps best situated as make-believe. Its success, in any case, is captured by the expressions of delight in the reactions of the spectators. The performance stages a form of hyperreality—the pleasure in watchers being watched. It seems, though, that very little is left to chance in this particular flash mob: some people in the film, as seen in figure 2.3, who are first shown as surprised passersby are later seen singing. It *might* just be possible that musicians could spontaneously come together to perform one of the great works of the Western canon—with Catalan lyrics. But it would be hard to imagine that they all were familiar with the radically abridged version that is presented in this video.

It is easy to criticize this phenomenon as the triumph of neoliberalism in the aesthetic realm, corresponding, perhaps, to Fukuyama's thesis of the end of history. This criticism would not be misguided, especially in the context of Banc Sabadell as the corporate instigator of this flash mob. But this critique is in danger of obscuring something equally important: the terms of this Beethoven 9 have fundamentally changed. As a performance it may be more productive to view it through the lens of situational art than as an attempt to reproduce the conditions of the concert hall. It is an installation that shares important features with Beethoven's Ninth,

FIGURE 2.3   Stills from the Sabadell flash mobs. (a) A girl gives a busking
double bass player a coin. (b) A passerby is surprised to hear the
music. (c) Later the same man is seen in the background joining
in with the other singers. (d) Tutti.

in that it pivots on the recognition of the "Ode to Joy," but it is
not fully coterminous with the symphony. Most importantly,
this rendition has a strong element of participation that is not
incidental but is rather a central feature: the amazed audiences are an integral component of the flash mob.

(c)

(d)

FIGURE 2.3 Continued

The real coup of the Ninth seems to be its ability to spur the imagination. The angle of memory may provide a lens through which we can view the "glossy" and the "grassroots" performances together, without having to pit felt authenticity against documentary correctness. Memory dispenses with both categories and appeals to an experiential, emotive, imaginary quality instead. In the realm of memory, the magic of the Ninth can rebind what custom strictly divided. As we saw before, the meaningfulness of Beethoven's Ninth has eclipsed any precise meaning that the symphony might elicit. A mere reminder, a memory, of this work, the *lieu de mémoire* of music par excellence, is all that is needed.

Beethoven's Ninth is, in a very real sense, the anthem of liberal democracy.[51] As the symphony has ascended to its global role, its details and subtleties have receded into the background. In that contested space between the proclaimed "end of history" and a history that is still very much marching on, the sounding of Beethoven's Ninth lends history a distinct experiential quality. History is being announced, not in retrospect but as it happens before our very eyes and ears. These renditions are media events—and this is true for both gloss and grassroots. It is no coincidence that we see some of the most media-savvy musicians, led by Leonard Bernstein, at the crest of this movement. But the Chilean protesters were just as aware that the musical message they chanted would resonate with a global audience. Instead of relishing the subtle pleasures of the unknowable, unconsummated symbols that Solomon uncovered in the work, we are in search of the thrill of the experience, of presence.

CHAPTER 3

MARKING HEARING

T HE NINTH HAD ALWAYS made unreasonable demands
on its listeners. Critics and audiences did not always
take kindly to this. It would be wrong to assume that the
symphony enjoyed its towering status in the musical repertoire right from its very conception. Its modern condition,
in which we have apparently forgotten how to listen to it,
is a fairly recent phenomenon. For much of the nineteenth
century the Ninth held a distinctly ambivalent position in
the symphonic canon. Important musicians in the mid-
nineteenth century, such as Felix Mendelssohn and Louis
Spohr, expressed their reservations about the Ninth, whose
gestures seemed too outlandish and whose form appeared
too enigmatic.[1] Were ill-prepared audiences ready to face
the challenges the music presented?[2]

Various attempts were made to rein in the Ninth. Careful emendations and adjustments, it was thought, might help to accommodate the work in the concert halls. The most sweeping of these adjustments was the practice, fairly widespread at one time, of programming just the first three movements and cutting the choral finale. But even on a less extreme level, throughout the nineteenth century and well into the twentieth, it was quite common for conductors to make editorial changes to the score, and some of them made significant alterations to the symphony. Richard Wagner's and Gustav Mahler's performance versions of the Ninth may be the most famous examples, but there are plenty of others.[3] A justification for those retouchings was not strictly required, since they fell under the discretion of the conductor who recreated the score in performance.

But there was also another reason that conductors used to justify their extensive wielding of the editorial pen, which (certainly in Wagner's case) was greater than the creative license generally taken with other symphonic works: Beethoven's deafness. The touching story from the premiere of the symphony in 1824 is well known, in which the contralto Caroline Unger, depicted in figure 3.1, turned the deaf composer around to face the auditorium after the performance so he could see the audience cheering and applauding his music.[4] Beethoven was at the height of his fame in Vienna, and the reviews there were generally marked by a predominantly reverential tone. But even then, a Viennese critic included a seed of doubt in his otherwise dithyrambic review about the effects of the composer's affliction, which would be echoed by other voices elsewhere:

FIGURE 3.1   The singer Caroline Unger (1803–77), the contralto of the first performance of Beethoven's Ninth Symphony. (Image: Beethoven-Haus Bonn.)

Even the most ardent worshippers and most fervent admirers of the composer are convinced that this truly unique finale would become even more incomparably imposing in a more concentrated shape, and that the composer himself would agree, had cruel fate not robbed him of the ability to hear his creation.[5]

Having tragically lost his hearing, the argument goes, Beethoven had no sense of what was musically possible or effective. Most of Beethoven's critics felt this was to the detriment of his work, but Wagner took a different tack. Beethoven's affliction, Wagner countered, had liberated the great composer from the constraints of regular music making and allowed his towering musical imagination free rein. Or, as Wagner put it, Beethoven's deafness "led him at last to an almost naïve disregard of the relation of the actual embodiment to the musical thought itself."[6] Either way, whether disabling or visionary, because of the composer's pathology, Beethoven's music required careful mediation. This opened up enormous interpretive space.

WAGNER'S NINTH

Wagner repeatedly credited the groundbreaking performances by his friend and father-in-law, the virtuoso pianist Franz Liszt, for making Beethoven's challenging late works intelligible and accessible. Likewise, he cited superior performances by (unnamed) German string quartets for finally making sense of Beethoven's enigmatic late quartets—what it took was for musicians to turn "their virtuosity to the correct rendering of these wondrous works."[7] It is not by accident that Wagner uses the emphatic adjective "correct" here (even though "felt right" may have been a better choice). For him, there was no question that these renditions of Beethoven's works corresponded exactly to their creator's conceptions.[8]

Wagner was convinced that his own performing version of the Ninth would similarly recreate, in a "correct" manner, Beethoven's artistic vision. This aesthetic position allowed him to blur the divisions between production and reproduction. From this perspective, the changes Wagner proposed were not so much editorial emendations or additions, a meddling with the score, as rather a clarification, which brought out the idea behind the music. One part of Wagner's emendations "updated" the scoring, taking into account the technical advances of musical instruments since Beethoven's days, such as keyed trumpets capable of playing an extended pitch range, and simplified the parts in fairly inconspicuous ways. But the other part of Wagner's revisions imprinted itself directly onto the presentation of the musical material. It is here that Beethoven's deafness manifested itself most clearly: Wagner argued that the score was only an indistinct representation of what went on in Beethoven's artistic mind, unfettered as it was by the shackles of hearing. What Wagner aimed to accomplish in his performance version was to resurrect and mediate the true artistic intention of the work, to bring out what Beethoven had been able to think in music but had been unable to express adequately in sounds, to fill in what was left out in the score and to channel Beethoven's artistic vision into musical sounds that lay audiences could understand.

The most controversial changes amounted to reworkings of entire passages in the first movement. Example 3.1 shows how Beethoven had split up the melodic line, with its cascading sixteenth notes, between the wind instruments (flute, oboes, clarinets) so that motivic fragments in a variety of instrumental colors coalesce into a melodic line. Thus, in example 3.1(a) the flute in m. 139 picks up the short motif that the oboe presented in m. 138, whereas the oboe part in m. 139 simply descends, without including the leap up to G that is heard in the flute part. Wagner, by contrast, felt he needed to preserve coherence and highlight an uninterrupted melodic flow, and this could best be done by assigning a continuous melody in its entirety to the same instrument. Here, in example 3.1(b), the oboe is given the whole melody with all the motivic details, while the flute part now merely seems to double it. A similar "stream-lining" of the parts can be observed in mm. 142–3 of the example. This "drastic marking of the melody,"[9] Wagner went on to explain, was key to the correct understanding of Beethoven's intention.

EXAMPLE 3.1   Beethoven, Symphony no. 9, first movement, mm. 138–45, (a) in the original version, and (b) flute and oboe parts in Wagner's reworkings (as reconstructed by Andreas Eichhorn).

BEETHOVEN'S SYMPHONY NO. 9

EXAMPLE 3.1 Continued

Wagner's version has been widely criticized, and with justification. Where Beethoven performed what is now called
durchbrochene Arbeit ("fragmented motivic work"), in which
the scintillations of the orchestral timbre formed an essential part of his symphonic palette, Wagner's "drastic" version
presented Beethoven's materials with broad brushstrokes
as one continuous line. True, Wagner's intrusion into the
score is significant, brutal even, and it reveals a misunderstanding of Beethoven's compositional aesthetics. There
can be no question that this was not Beethoven's intention,
deafness or not. However, from the perspective of communication, Wagner may have had a point: Wagner availed
himself of a psychological principle that is now known as
auditory scene analysis, which states that we are much more
likely to perceive a series of events as an overriding whole
if the instrumental timbres in which they are presented are
continuous. In other words, Wagner's concern was with
the lack of melodic clarity—and his retouchings certainly
streamline Beethoven's version to bring out the melodic flow.

It should not surprise us that Wagner, yet again, credited Liszt with this realization; he referenced specifically Liszt's own piano arrangement of the Ninth.[10] Andreas Eichhorn has shown that this is more than a polite tip of the hat. As seen in example 3.2, Liszt's arrangement—in contrast to Wagner's own piano version, which is both more literal and clunkier—omits certain details of the orchestral texture in order to privilege the smooth melodic flow, and it is this feature that Wagner orchestrates in his retouchings.[11] Normally in the nineteenth century piano arrangements were thought to be deficient—they were frequently faulted for their "monochromatic" rendering of the full orchestral experience, much like the copper engravings, found in countless nineteenth-century middle-class homes, that offered serviceable (if colorless) reproductions of oil paintings by the great masters to hang on domestic walls.[12] Here Wagner actually turned this reproach into an advantage: after all, it was Liszt's piano arrangement of the Ninth that first allowed him to understand the true nature of Beethoven's music. Or at least, this is what he believed it did. Liszt's piano arrangement allowed him to see *through* the orchestration.

Whatever we think about the legitimacy of Wagner's edition—and the polarities of documentary correctness versus felt authenticity loom large again—it clearly takes great liberties in its reading of the work. Wagner sought to bring out an inner greatness of the work, that is, certain structural features that are inherent in the music but may be hidden, partly because of Beethoven's deafness. Of course, this very deafness, or so Wagner was convinced, had allowed Beethoven to progress to an artistic stage far ahead of his time. In a word: his deafness had made Beethoven great.[13]

Wagner could well describe his role in this intervention as a medium. The self-assurance with which he talks about restoring Beethoven's "correct" intentions may conjure up the mystical kind of medium, through and by means of which posterity is enabled to communicate with the dead.[14] But the more modern kind of medium, a technology that channels and transmits information across time and space, is also not far off. In either case, the mediation creates a wholly new listening experience.

MONUMENTS OLD AND NEW: ENTER 9 BEET STRETCH

Wagner's editorial changes, jettisoning motivic subtleties in favor of a clear melodic outline, painted with a broad brushstroke, were efforts to monumentalize the Ninth. From our perspective, such efforts seem like gilding the lily, but they may receive some justification from the ambivalence in the mid-nineteenth century vis-à-vis Beethoven's final symphony. At the heart of the concept of monumentality is, in musicologist Carl Dahlhaus's words, "a simplicity that stands up to being stated emphatically, without collapsing in empty rhetoric."[15] Others point out that monuments aim to overwhelm rather than persuade; the message that monuments convey is not subtle but forceful. This is why the clear intelligibility of the melodic line trumped the intricacy of Beethoven's motivic work in Wagner's version.

At the most basic level, the cultural function of monuments is to articulate history.[16] But not everybody shows as much confidence in monumentality as Dahlhaus does. This drive toward simple and forceful messaging is also one of the reasons monumentality is often regarded with considerable suspicion, especially in light of the dubious political ends to which it has been put by totalitarian and imperialist regimes. The most immediate and eye-catching facet of which monumentality avails itself is scale, the idea that an inner greatness must be made manifest by means of outsize proportions. As Thomas Mann tartly commented, a propos of Richard Wagner, somehow size came to be seen as the natural corollary of ethical grandeur.[17] The overwhelming effect of monumental art, its ability to inspire awe, which sometimes seems to assume hypnotic powers, reeks of ideology, as was borne out again and again over the course of the twentieth century.

The concept of monumentality, with all its seductive power, made a major comeback in the closing years of the twentieth century, particularly after the fall of the Berlin Wall. As the cultural historian Andreas Huyssen has astutely observed, this contemporary version of monumentality, in the wake of 1989, is significantly different from its more bombastic nineteenth-century counterpart in one important respect—this new monumentality is, as it were, served with a postmodern twist.[18] It retains the outsize proportions and simple, easily consumable structures familiar from its nineteenth-century precursor, but it shuns the gothic massiveness that was the traditional garb of monumental art. From this perspective, it is better understood as a form of monumentality that is simultaneously "anti-monumental"—toying instead with impermanence, concealment, virtuality. In this playful, virtual guise, this new monumentality ultimately reaches a public willing to re-engage in a guilty pleasure. Needless to say, the digital realm—especially the internet, which was expanded to commercial traffic in the 1990s—opened up all sorts of new possibilities, allowing monumentality to migrate, in Huyssen's words, "from the real into the image, from the material into the immaterial, and ultimately into the digitized computer bank."[19] This virtual kind of monumentality has no material existence, but it is everywhere.

Leif Inge's *9 Beet Stretch*, the vastly decelerated digital artwork we encountered in chapter 1, is an adaptation of the Ninth that can be understood fairly straightforwardly in the terms that Huyssen has laid out for his notion of monumentality. In many ways it is less intrusive than Wagner's nineteenth-century adaptation, in that it does not tinker with Beethoven's score, even if the final product is much more "drastic" than even Wagner's rescoring. But let's not get ahead of ourselves; let's first take a look at the piece itself. Leif Inge, a self-described idea-based artist, offers a "score" of 9 *Beet Stretch*—his opus 5—that consists of the following verbal instructions:

> A recording of Beethoven's 9th Symphony is to be stretched to 24 hours, with no pitch distortion. For installation or performance, use either supplied material or augment any full length digital recording of Beethoven's 9th symphony. As the length of the source recordings varies, so will the ratio of the augmentation vary to reach the full 24 hours length. . . . There is a version of 9 Beet Stretch for each recording available of Beethoven's 9th symphony.[20]

What is left tantalizingly unclear is to which genre 9 *Beet Stretch* belongs. The piece hovers somewhere in the space between sound installation, electroacoustic performance, and ambient soundscape.[21] If it is a performance, is it still a performance of Beethoven's Ninth, or is there a difference if it is a performance of a recording of Beethoven's Ninth?

9 *Beet Stretch* was first unveiled—if that's the right word—at the Kupfer Ironworks in Madison, Wisconsin, on April 16–17, 2004. It made quite a splash, perhaps more in the popular media than in the musical world. The reasons this piece piqued the popular imagination are obvious: this is a piece of sounding art that has Beethoven's name attached to it, a name that will mean something to everybody, even if they are connoisseurs neither of concert music nor of digital sound installations.

Besides the performances of Leif Inge's 9 *Beet Stretch* in specific locations all over the world, the piece can be downloaded or streamed from a number of websites, and it is also available in excerpts on the companion website for this book ▶. Leif Inge's realization is based on a recording of Beethoven's Ninth by the Hungarian conductor Béla Drahos and the Nicolaus Esterházy Sinfonia and Chorus, issued by the low-cost Naxos label. This choice seems to underline a point: this is not one of the iconic recordings of Beethoven's Ninth—not Furtwängler's, not Karajan's, not Toscanini's Ninth—but one from a label that specializes in making a wide range of music available while paying relatively little attention to the name recognition of its performers and conductors.[22] As Leif Inge underscores, the source recording itself plays a role only insofar as it is the material for the stretched-out version, and it is eminently replaceable.

What is foregrounded instead is the sounding materiality of the music. Using granulation software, Leif Inge slows down the recording by a factor of 22.15, so as to last twenty-four hours exactly. In the streamed version of the installation, the piece is on permanent loop and always starts at 6:18 p.m. Central European Time, apparently the time of sunset in Vienna on March 26, 1827, Beethoven's death day.[23] This is an arbitrary time, to be sure, but one that can be reconstructed with a high degree of accuracy and that firmly anchors the piece in the time and place in the orbit of its conception.

To understand what is going on here, we have to delve a little deeper into the problem of slowing music down. Anyone who remembers playing records using turntables will know what it means to speed up an LP from the usual 33 1/3 rpm to 78, or to slow down singles from their typical 45 rpm to 33 1/3: accelerating a vocal recording produces a high-pitched Chipmunks voice, while decelerating produces a low voice-from-beyond-the-grave. Speed and pitch are inextricably coupled. If an analog recording is played at the wrong speed, it is not just the rhythms that are affected but the pitch levels as well. The reason for this coupling is that both pitches—or rather their acoustical correlate, frequencies—and rhythms are temporal functions.[24]

It is only in the digital realm that the problem of uncoupling pitches from rhythms can be successfully tackled, by means of the process of granular synthesis, which is now quite common but was fairly revolutionary in 2002.[25] We can best imagine granular synthesis as a splicing of the digitized soundwave into minuscule temporal units, individual grains or instants lasting only a few milliseconds, each preserving the pitch-, timbre- and loudness-related components of the sounds. Each slice of time is then replicated for as many times as is necessary, so that the resulting sounds happen in slower succession, but their pitch levels—and, to a large extent, their timbres—are preserved.[26] In the case of 9 *Beet Stretch*, the individual instants of the Béla Drahos recording were replicated a sufficient number of times to extend the duration of their original sounding by a factor of 22.15. Then they were put back together again, as it were. In this way, the frequency information within each slice of time is preserved, while the temporal duration of each sound is stretched out. Sound example 3.1 on the companion website plays a passage from the start of the fugato of the Scherzo, as shown in example 3.3. In a standard performance this passage lasts no more than few seconds, in this decelerated version the sinewy counterpoint is turned into several minutes of viscous sound, slowly trickling by the listener as a short eternity.

EXAMPLE 3.3   Beethoven, Symphony no. 9, second movement, mm. 177–85.

Critics of the first performances of this work had a field day putting into words what they had been hearing. The resulting slow sounds have been described as "cosmic" or "frozen," reaching "new heights of beauty," "vast fields of sound," with "gossamer lines" and "dissonances and suspensions tak[ing] forever to melt," a "nightmarish avalanche," and a "cascade of quivering overtones."[27] Whatever the preferred metaphor, there is general agreement that the resulting sounds most closely resemble ambient music—not only that but "high-class ambient music."[28]

The piece moves at a pace that is simply too slow for listeners to successfully follow melodies, progressions, or contours most of the time. The tones, chords, and sonorities of the recording unfold in grainy, sometimes mushy, slowness. The glacial passage of the music makes it impossible to discern an underlying pulse. Themes, phrases, motives—the normal markers of musical form—are all but unrecognizable at this slow speed. Only the most salient musical events, such as the bare descending fourths and fifths of the opening or the sharp dotted timpani rhythms from the Scherzo, can just about be recognized. Beginning, middle, and end have been erased by the work's looped existence on the internet, which suggests that it is neither likely nor necessary that we will listen to the piece from beginning to end.[29] (Leif Inge confessed that he has never listened to the whole piece from beginning to end in one sitting.) All aspects of form invariably recede into the background at this glacial speed.[30]

What moves into center stage instead are the smallest details of the performance, which are all but unnoticeable at the speed of a typical performance of Beethoven's Ninth. One critic even observed how the scraping rasp of horsehair against the violin string, "sustained instead of allowed to bounce by," had a "noticeable fingernail-on-the-blackboard quality."[31] Listening to this recording is the equivalent of looking through a microscope: it brings tiny details into focus and, what is more, shifts the entire register of perception so as to open up a completely new level of observation.

It is particularly the overlaps between harmonic changes, the moves from one chord to the next, that stand out in this slow version as harshly grating dissonances. This is not because the Nicolaus Esterházy Sinfonia might not be up to the task of performing the work, but rather because it is humanly impossible for each member of a large symphony orchestra to move from one note to the next at exactly the same pace; tiny individual variations will always exist. This is particularly noticeable in the short passage depicted in example 3.3 above (and decelerated in audio example 1 ▶), with its rapid note changes and contrapuntal textures.

Whereas in a conventional listening experience these inaccuracies occupy fractions of seconds, the slowed-down version presents them as long and distinctly audible sonic events. These stretched-out moments are an artifact of granular synthesis, whenever a slice of time cuts through a typically fleeting moment during which two adjacent chords are sounded simultaneously. Because of their highly dissonant character, it is these moments *between* chords that stand out of the musical tapestry. In a word, this is music made at the interstices.

The experience of the slowness of *9 Beet Stretch* has been described as a "metabolic shift in listening," causing one commentator to feel catapulted "inside the sounds, inside the harmonies, and hence inside Beethoven's head."[32] (The idea of recreational drug consumption, and its effects on perception, is never far from these kinds of comments.) *9 Beet Stretch*, he continued to enthuse, may be "the closest we can ever come to experiencing what the deaf Beethoven heard, or experienced, in his head."[33] It is perhaps not too surprising that associations with Beethoven's deafness should suggest themselves. It is not immediately obvious, though, how exactly a vastly slowed-down sense of temporality should be the sonic correlate of deafness, except perhaps in the sense that the mental image of the sound world of his composition was not bound to the limitations of linear time. Still, when musicians in the nineteenth and twentieth centuries such as Johannes Brahms and Heinrich Schenker prized the perfection of silent score reading over an actual performance, one imagines this wasn't quite what they had in mind.[34]

MONUMENTALIZING THE NINTH

9 Beet Stretch presents a different aspect of the renewed culture of monumentality of Beethoven's Ninth during the 1990s and 2000s, though its particular sound world sets the piece apart from the self-consciously historic performances of the time. Its monumentality stands alone, like the mysterious black monolith from Stanley Kubrick's celebrated film *2001: A Space Odyssey* (1968). It is all surface, and yet inscrutable. Its curious sounds offer a novel response to the challenge of what there is left to be heard in a Ninth that is otherwise all too easily accommodated. This specific performance in the digital realm allows us to hear the symphony with fresh ears. The radically different listening experience challenges us to think about the symphony anew.

But can we actually still speak of the Ninth if it doesn't sound anything like the symphony we know? This is the moment to bring back our imaginary skeptic from the introduction. We can answer with reference to the philosopher Nelson Goodman, who presented perhaps the most stringent criteria to define the work of music: we can only speak of a performance of the work, he argued, if all the pitch relations and all the rhythmic relations are accurately rendered.[35] In other words, if one note is played wrong, it no longer constitutes a performance of the work. Musicians have long complained that this definition is pedantic, unrealistic, and missing the point, in that it focuses on formal aspects that leave out precisely what makes a performance musical.[36] Goodman agrees that this definition is not helpful to musicians; his motivations are philosophical.[37] What is interesting for our purposes is that *9 Beet Stretch* is fully compliant with Goodman's criteria: as long as Drahos's performance constitutes a rendition of Beethoven's Ninth, *9 Beet Stretch* does as well. The time needed for a performance, or our ability to recognize the musical structures perceptually, does not play a part. This philosophical approach, despite its obvious shortcomings for musicians, lays out a framework in which we can productively grapple with the relationship between Beethoven's Ninth and *9 Beet Stretch* and in which this digital monument, this "composition" in Attali's sense, can shed a light on the significance of Beethoven's Ninth in the new millennium.

9 Beet Stretch can best be understood as a performance twice removed. The stretched-out performance is based on a recording of Beethoven's Ninth Symphony.[38] The "score" of *9 Beet Stretch* is the CD recording, in figure 3.2, in the same way that the printed score of Beethoven's Ninth Symphony forms the basis of the performance by the Esterházy Sinfonia. (This is in addition to Leif Inge's instructions on how to produce this piece, which, as we saw, constitutes in itself a kind of "score.") Reviewers of *9 Beet Stretch* were right on the mark, in more ways than one, when they called the piece a "masterpiece of a masterpiece."[39]

Leif Inge explained: "By stretching Beethoven's Ninth I don't only stretch a piece of music, I stretch music history."[40] His work is very much concerned with the cultural status of Beethoven's work in the popular imagination. The "score" of *9 Beet Stretch* ends, perhaps with tongue in cheek, with the remark: "If . . . for any reason [it] is hard to obtain a copy of Beethoven's 9th symphony, please use Wolfgang Amadeus Mozart's Requiem."[41] The idea that the Ninth is exchangeable with Mozart's Requiem underscores nothing

BEETHOVEN

DDD
8.553478

Symphony No. 9 "Choral"

Papian • Donose • Fink • Otelli
Nicolaus Esterházy Sinfonia and Chorus
Béla Drahos

FIGURE 3.2   Beethoven, Symphony no. 9, recording no. 8553478, with Béla
Drahos and the Nicolaus Esterházy Sinfonia (Naxos), the
"score" on which Leif Inge's realization of *9 Beet Stretch* is
based.

so much as the cultural capital associated with the source—
in the unlikely event, in our media-saturated world, that
no recording of the Ninth is available, one canonical work
can be substituted for another. By stretching the sounds of
Beethoven's Ninth almost beyond comprehensibility, he is
making an audible cultural commentary. The whole day,
every day, is filled with the sounds of the Ninth. It is simply

too big, in every sense, to be taken in at once. Our (digital) world is so suffused with the Ninth that we can afford—indeed, we are encouraged—to tune in and out. Leif Inge's work, like Beethoven's own, constantly surrounds us. At the same time, *9 Beet Stretch* lets us hear a soundworld that we have never encountered before. These are, in a very literal way, unheard-of sounds.

CHAPTER 4

MARKING TIME

T HE MILLENNIUM IS A strange psychological affair. It is not exactly historical; we could question whether it really constitutes an event. Nothing actually happens, other than the turn of all the digits of one long number into another one—from 23:59:59 12/31/1999 to 00:00:00 01/01/2000. In this excitement over numbers, only pedants would try to remind the rest of the world that the actual new millennium wouldn't technically start until January 1, 2001. While logically correct, however, this later date fails to capture the magic of numbers; the psychological significance of the moment was inextricably bound up with the moment time turned from 1999 to 2000.

The tremendous effect of this change, known as Y2K, could easily be called mass-hypnotic. A significant number of people were seriously concerned our technological world would become catastrophically disrupted overnight, by the simple oversight of programmers to account for the switch from 99 to 00 in the internal clocks of ubiquitous computer chips. On this fateful day, it was predicted, life-saving hospital machinery would spontaneously shut down, defense systems would critically fail, planes would fall out of the sky. The world waited with bated breath to see if we would live to see the other side of Y2K.

Needless to say, not all New Year celebrations in 2000 were so apocalyptic in spirit. For most people the millennial turn was an occasion to celebrate in grand style. It also offered an opportunity for extensive reflections on the past millennium and musings on the one to come. Years, decades, centuries, millennia bend time from a linear process into quasi-circular phenomena with beginnings and endings. The Ninth is tightly bound up with many such celebrations marking time. The moment when time folds in on itself, when we look back from the present to reflect on the year that is ending, is marked with performances of the Ninth in various parts of the world, from the solemn concert performances in German-speaking Europe to the massed sing-alongs of *daiku* in Japan. And when time folded in on itself in the most spectacular way, at the turn of the millennium, it was obvious that Beethoven's Ninth had a big role to play.

MILLENNIAL MUSIC

Music, as the temporal art par excellence, played a major part in the millennial celebrations, beyond just performances of Beethoven's Ninth. A number of important compositions and sound installations were launched in or around 2000, to mark this important moment in time. Perhaps the best-known piece of "millennial music" is the Halberstadt John Cage Organ project (2001).[1] This performance, based on John Cage's composition *ASLSP/Organ*[2] (1987) takes the title—"As SLow aS Possible"—rather literally: the rendition in the church of St. Burchardi in the small German town of Halberstadt will take 639 years. The length of the performance was based on the age of the old organ in the church, installed in 1361, which finally needed to be replaced in year 2000. This monumental rendition of the piece, which typically lasts somewhere between a few minutes and over an hour in conventional performances, began with a full year and a half of silence.[2] In preparation for each sound change, the new organ pipes are added as necessary. Needless to say, a performance that operates in these dimensions cannot rely on a human performer: weights attached to the keys hold them down and sound the organ for a near eternity.

The piece *Longplayer* (1999) by Jem Finer, a founding member of the Celtic punk band the Pogues, will even last a full thousand years, from New Year's 2000 to New Year's 2999. Scored for Tibetan sound bowls, "bronze-age oscillators,"[3] as Finer calls them jokingly, and worked out in accordance with a computer algorithm, the piece is located on the zero meridian in Greenwich, England, that is, on the geographic line that acts as a reference for the global divisions into time zones. From there it can be heard at listening stations all over the world, from San Francisco to Sydney. The irony that the computer technology that makes this piece possible will be outdated long before the end of the composition has been reached is not lost on Finer.

But no millennial musical event comes even close to the majestic temporal dimensions in which the *Clock of the Long Now* operates. Devised by the computer engineer Danny Hillis and first displayed, as a prototype, at the Science Museum in London, the clock is supposed to keep time for ten thousand years—a myriad. Hillis explained his idea in 1993:

> I think it is time for us to start a long-term project that gets people thinking past the mental barrier of the Millennium. I would like to propose a large (think Stonehenge) mechanical clock, powered by seasonal temperature changes. It ticks once a year, bongs once a century, and the cuckoo comes out every millennium.[4]

The *Clock of the Long Now* began its work on December 31, 1999, just in time to ring in the new millennium. For the ten-thousand-year clock, Y2K is known as 02000. Strictly speaking, the fifth digit would only be necessary if we are thinking about a duration of 100,000 years (99,999+1), but the main point is to set its timescale off, in a visually striking way, from the standard mode of marking time. Similarly, there is no inherent reason why the clock should not tick every second (ca. 315,569,520,000 times)[5] instead of making noises at such a infrequent rate—except for the powerful psychological satisfaction that underscores the enormous scale of the project by means of majestic slowness.

The symbolic power of the whole project cannot be underestimated. As the novelist Michael Chabon points out, it does not matter whether the clock will really run for that amount of time, or indeed whether humanity will be there to witness the end of this long period: what matters is that it helps us conceptualize the imagined connection between us and the most distant past and future.[6] It is no coincidence that Hillis imagines his timepiece as a gigantic cuckoo clock—it is the very concreteness of the material object that allows us to begin to grapple with concepts that would otherwise lie far beyond our comprehension.

All these millennial projects are concerned with immense durations. In the field of music, slowness is one important way of achieving temporal length, but it is far from the only one. (Finer's *Longplayer*, for instance, is certainly long, but not particularly slow.) What matters in these millennial pieces, no matter how their sublime lengths are generated, is the contemplation of the long time spans that they articulate. The "long now" describes the imagined connection between the present and the most distant past and future. Fittingly, the concept of the long now was developed by the musician Brian Eno, who is acutely aware, as a composer and music producer, of the power of temporality.[7]

And this distant future is hopeful. The organizers at Halberstadt view their extremely slow performance as a "musical apple tree," a "symbol of confidence in the future."[8] (The image of the apple tree alludes to a popular German aphorism, usually ascribed to Martin Luther: "If I knew that the world were to end tomorrow, I would plant an apple tree today.") Similarly, the *Clock of the Long Now* is an invitation to look into the future with optimism. The manifest object of the clock gives material shape to an otherwise unfathomable idea. Under the impression of the clock, the writer Michael Chabon pictures the unknowable future and the promises that the world holds ten thousand years from now. This is no easy task, he concedes, especially given that human

extinction over that period is a near certainty.[9] But we ultimately bear an obligation toward our children to envision
that future. Parents cannot but be optimists; they simply have
no choice in this matter. The very decision to have children
and to love them, Chabon explains, means that we are bet-
ting on the future. He recalls a conversation with his eight-
year-old son: "'Will there really be people then, Dad?'—'Yes,'
I told him without hesitation, 'there will.'"[10]

THE NINTH AS TEMPORAL UNIT

Leif Inge's 9 *Beet Stretch*, which was first generated in 2002
in an online-only version, belongs in this group of millennial musical events, even though its timescale appears relatively modest when compared with these musical pieces on
the most gigantic scale. The duration of the installation, at
exactly twenty-four hours, definitely exceeds our normal
attention span. There is something orderly about the length
of twenty-four hours, one of our standard measurements
of time, even if stretching a recording of Beethoven's Ninth
Symphony over a span of a whole day may still seem like
an arbitrary decision. Once we start digging, however, we
remember that thinking about Beethoven's Ninth, especially
a CD recording of Beethoven's Ninth Symphony, in the context of measurements of time is anything but arbitrary.

The story of how Beethoven's Ninth was used to determine the temporal format of the CD around 1980 is widely
known. Originally developed jointly by the Dutch mul-
tinational electronics company Philips and its Japanese
rival Sony, CD technology was a rare occasion of two
international competitors collaborating on a joint format.

The vice president of Sony, Norio Ohga, so the story goes, was a big fan of *daiku*.[11] Those who grew up with gramophone records will remember that the symphony could only be fitted awkwardly onto three record sides, which meant that any double album had to be coupled with another shorter work to fill the fourth side. The Beethoven-loving executive had requested that the new medium be made long enough to accommodate the entire symphony on one disc; the slowest known recording of Beethoven's Ninth Symphony in existence, Furtwängler's 1951 performance, required just under seventy-five minutes' playing time. And so, the story concludes, it was done. Originally the diameter of the disc, at 115 mm, was chosen to correspond to the diagonal length of a cassette tape, but it was decided in May 1980—in the eleventh hour—to augment the size to 120 mm across, and to set the playing time at seventy-five minutes.

In reality, the presence of Beethoven lovers in the inner circle of Sony management was probably not the only reason why a slightly longer (and physically larger) format was favored.[12] Philips, which had produced the prototype, was slightly ahead with their CD production facilities. Drawing attention to the need for a new, slightly longer format was an elegant way to make sure that Sony would have some more time to catch up. And what better way to allow everybody to save face than by presenting this crucial change to the public in terms of high cultural standards? Whatever the specifics of the underlying competition in a global market, the need to accommodate Beethoven's Ninth Symphony has become the officially sanctioned rationale, promoted by both companies. Philips, whimsically, even credited the composer himself: "The playing time was determined posthumously by Beethoven."[13] From this perspective, the length of twenty-four hours is as much a standard measurement of time as is Beethoven's Ninth Symphony. One temporal unit is expanded into another. Time slows down.

TIME AXIS MANIPULATION

If media are integral to this story—if it makes a difference whether Beethoven's music is stored on manuscript paper, the grooves of a gramophone recording, the magnetic charges of reel-to-reel tape, or the zeros and ones of binary code—we can think of sound media as forms of inscription, kinds of writing. The German philosopher Sybille Krämer argues that the manipulation of time plays a vital and often overlooked role in technical media. She offers a radical definition of media, as "practices that use strategies of spatialization to enable one to manipulate the order of things that progress in time."[14] Krämer understands media not as technological objects, a CD player or a gramophone, but as what she calls cultural techniques, by which she means very basic activities, such as writing, counting, or collecting.[15] The idea of writing is central here, and we can easily adapt it to musical writing: when we write—in the most general terms—we spell words in letters and transform sounds into recognizable objects in spatial sequences on the page.

This practice is called time axis manipulation. "By shifting the chronological order of time," Krämer explains, "to the parallel order of space—and spaces are things that can principally be restructured—written media become elementary forms that not only allow temporal order to be stored but also to be manipulated or reversed."[16] It is easy to see how this would work in musical notation: the notes in a musical passage can easily be reversed in performance by playing them backwards. It would be much harder to do this purely based on hearing the sound of the original passage, without any visual—spatialized—aids. For example, turning to the opening of the slow movement, Pieter van den Toorn's Schenkerian analysis, in example 4.1, points out how the melody and the bass line are a precise inversion of each other and how the same melodic three-note figure is then repeated in the bass register. It is easy to see in his analytical notation how this works, moved to the parallel order of space, though it would be much harder to perceive those relations exclusively from hearing the music in time.

EXAMPLE 4.1 Beethoven, Symphony no. 9, third movement, opening. Pieter van den Toorn's Schenkerian analysis of the score points toward motivic connections, highlighted in boxes, between melody and bass.

Reversal is only the most obvious form of manipulating the recall of events on the basis of spatialization, as it starkly juxtaposes the visual and aural dimensions. An even more basic version of such time axis manipulation would be to slow down the music; this form of manipulation is so fundamental to our musical experience that we would not even register it as such. This is just, we might think, what music does naturally. This is correct if we are talking about "live" performance, where the specific temporal dimension is relatively flexible, as long as the relative durations of the tones—the rhythms—remain accurate.

Things are a little different when we move to recording technology, and this is where the principles of time axis manipulation get interesting. A recording, whether analog or digital, also spatializes time, with one important difference: musical notation functions as a kind of filter that only allows certain units (that is, musical signs that can be expressed as note values, with stems, flags, or beams, with distinct pitches along the five lines and four spaces that make up our notation system) to be processed, and it inhibits everything else, simply because it cannot be notated adequately. By contrast, in a recording any sound, any noise, even a music stand falling over in the middle of the performance, becomes part of the recorded sound, irrespective of whether it is in the score or not.[17] A recording is still a form of writing, but of a fundamentally different kind. It is not notes but tones—that is, soundwaves themselves—that are captured in the recording. Tones are no longer discrete events but part of a continuous sound event that is encoded in the recording. In other words, the "phonograph inscribes not the spirit of music but its body, its acoustic being."[18] If a recording is played backwards, the entire soundwave engraved in the gramophone record or the binary code stored on a CD or in an MP3 is reversed. And, as a further consequence of this different kind of musical writing, the musical text that is recorded is no longer accessible to a musical performer, no longer legible with the naked eye, but must be decoded by machines.

TIME FOLDING IN ON ITSELF

The idea of time axis manipulation was primarily developed with the view to technological forms of writing—its starting point is very much the accelerated "Chipmunks voice" on the record player that never failed to amuse children. But, as we saw, the tools of time axis manipulation extend much further and can also be brought to bear on Beethoven's score. For a striking example, let's turn to the opening pages of the last movement in the score of Beethoven's Ninth Symphony. In these measures, famously, time folds in on itself. The recall of the themes of the earlier movements is a theatrical moment that plays with the temporal order of the music. One can easily read these flashbacks as a none-too-subtle sign that the basic unit of the symphony is not the individual movement, but that meaning resides in the symphony as a whole. A classic text by George Grove offers an interpretation along these lines:

> And then a remarkable passage occurs in which Beethoven passes in review each of the preceding three movements, as if to see whether [any] of them will suit for his *Finale*. . . . Hitherto, in the three orchestral movements, Beethoven has been depicting "Joy" in his own proper character: first, as part of the complex life of the individual man; secondly, for the world at large; thirdly, in all the ideal hues that art can throw over it. He has now to illustrate what Schiller intended in his Ode.[19]

For Grove, there is a clear succession encompassing ever greater entities: from the individual, to the world, to an ideal, and finally culminating in the universal distinctness of Schiller's poetry. It is understandable, and symptomatic of the nineteenth century in which Grove wrote, that he assigns the principal agency of this progression to the composer himself. In this interpretation, Beethoven uses the introduction of the final movement effectively to compose out the compositional choices he made in writing this symphony.

Grove's interpretation that Beethoven is in search of the appropriate angle of joy for the final movement is based on the famous introductory lines of the baritone solo: "O friends, not these tones! But let us sound more pleasant and joyful ones." (O Freunde, nicht diese Töne! Sondern lasst uns angenehmere anstimmen, und freudenvollere.) From musicologist Gustav Nottebohm's pioneering study of the sketches, we know, moreover, that the instrumental recitatives that punctuate the recall of earlier themes were at one stage conceived as texted passages, with verbal commentaries on each theme immediately after it is sounded.[20] These texted passages, transcribed in example 4.2, underscore that each theme from an earlier movement is rejected as insufficient: "Oh no, not this. Something else, something pleasant I demand," "Nor this. It's not better, only a little more cheerful," and "This, too, is too tender. We must look for something vivacious." Only the "Joy" theme passes muster: "That's it. Ha, now it is found." It remains ambiguous, however, to whom this voice belongs: Beethoven? An independent narrator? A personified musical self-consciousness? These questions are compounded by Beethoven's decision to cut these texted recitatives from the final version. Are the discarded commentaries no longer part of the music? Does their meaning still resonate, though the words are now erased?

EXAMPLE 4.2   Nottebohm's transcription of the sketches to the Finale,
from Landsberg 8/2 (Staatsbibliothek zu Berlin/Preußischer
Kulturbesitz), with running commentary on the music.

From the perspective of time, we could also interpret the music of the flashback as existing on a different plane than the recitatives: the recalled themes are mimetic; they are representations, reminiscences of the music heard earlier that stand outside of the regular narrative flow of the symphony. This is the moment when the music seems to become self-conscious of its existence as music—when it becomes, as it were, audible to itself as music. It is this separate existence that makes possible a commentary on these recalled themes, whether it is explicitly clothed in sung words, as suggested by the earlier sketches, or subsumed in instrumental recitative, as in the final version.

The principle of time axis manipulation allows us to dig deeper into this temporal perspective on the music. When viewed, on the most fundamental level, as a data stream, the recall of earlier themes is relatively easy to explain. The spatialized music does not need to follow the chronological order of temporal flow. (If we want a concrete technological model, we can perhaps imagine this in terms of the "scan function" of early CD players, where the first few seconds of each track were sounded in order, as a sounding indexing function. Obviously this is not to suggest that Beethoven had a CD player in mind, just that this technology may open a way for us to conceptualize what is going on. Media theorists use the term "recursion" for this kind of reiteration at another level—a self-similarity, a mise en abyme.[21]) Beethoven's score simulates such an effect within the medium of musical notation, rather than by digital or mechanical means. Or, if we prefer a descriptive term that is less explicitly technological, we might call these passages, with Dutch historian Johan Huizinga, "ecstatic time"—a time that is removed from our everyday temporal experience and stands outside of its regular flow.[22]

But we should take this one step further. It is striking that the number of measures recalled is (loosely) inversely proportional to the tempo of the movements: the Allegro sounds nine measures, the Vivace eight, whereas the Adagio recaptures a mere two measures plus one beat before breaking off. That is to say, the recall seems to be based less on thematic units and more on fixed temporal durations: each of the three individual moments of recall last roughly the same time in performance.

What is more, in the recall the temporal unfolding of the thematic material is foreshortened. Whereas in the original movements the themes tend to emerge gradually, in the recall they are fully present. The orchestration tends to be similarly streamlined, though never so much that a listener who does not have a score in front of him- or herself would notice the modifications. In a word, these flashbacks are quite different from the motivic techniques that Beethoven employs so skillfully in his compositions and that provide coherence within and across his movements.[23] Beethoven is not a copyist here but a sound engineer: it is not the notes that are being recalled but the memory of their sound.

The most drastic change of the recall from the earlier appearance it references is that of the first movement, in example 4.3. Despite the instantly recognizable sound, the music that is recalled here in fact never appeared in this form in the earlier movement. To be sure, the recall gestures toward the creatio ex nihilo, the gradual assemblage of the theme out of motivic fragments. But here the music does not start out of primordial silence; the motivic progress is

EXAMPLE 4.3 Beethoven, Symphony no. 9, fourth movement, mm. 30–38. (Cf. Examples 1.1 and 1.3.)

supported throughout by a sustained bass note C-sharp, which has the effect of framing the passage in a first-inversion chord. We know this gesture too: it is a reference not to the very opening but rather to its return in the recapitulation (there as a D-major chord in first inversion). Unlike the shattering fortissimo of the recapitulation, however, this recall remains in pianissimo throughout. The orchestration is similarly adjusted and subtly compacted: the winds do not enter gradually here, as they did at the beginning of the symphony, but they softly sustain the prevailing A-major harmony; where in the first movement violas and double basses participate in the sounding of the motivic fragments, their rhythms are taken up here, almost by allusion, by bassoon, trumpets, and timpani. The recall is a simulacrum, a flashback to an idealized version, sounding memories of earlier occurrences that never existed in the first place.

The final movement in Beethoven's symphony returns us to bygone times in a way that is not possible in our normal experience of chronological time but that can, and does, happen in music. The principle of time axis manipulation that makes this possible can exist in any medium, whether it is a score or a digital recording. The main difference is that in score format—where the spatialization of temporality is the norm—we tend not to draw attention to time axis manipulation, which assumes an air of normalcy as a consequence. It requires a special moment in the music in which sounds from earlier movements are recreated in the wrong context, disrupting the linearity of our experience, to draw our attention to its capacity to manipulate time in this way. Heard from this perspective, the sounds do not have to function as a sign waiting to be decoded within a symphonic totality, but they can also be understood as signals that help us come to terms with the profound question of how time—and our experience of it—operates. In this way, we can hear the Ninth, itself a distinct unit of time, folding time before our very ears.

CHAPTER 5

MARKING FORM

IF WE TRY TO attend to questions of form while listening to *9 Beet Stretch*, the extreme deceleration of the music has a disorienting effect, making it pass at a pace so slow as to raise the question of whether it has a pace at all. The musical "now," that is, our sense of where we are within the metric organization of the music, can either be imagined as vastly expanded—by a factor of 22.15, to be precise, whatever that may mean for an indefinite quantity such as "now"—or as completely vanished in the indistinguishable wash of sound. Either way, the experience of these sounds is one of formlessness. While this seems like a fairly uncontroversial statement, certainly as regards *9 Beet Stretch*, it poses some interesting questions. Would or wouldn't this have implications for our understanding of the form of Beethoven's Ninth as well? To put it provocatively, for the sake of the argument, an analysis of the structure of *9 Beet Stretch* that is largely indifferent to questions of tempo or performance—such as a harmonic analysis in terms of Roman numerals, or a Schenkerian analysis—should technically be identical with the analysis of the symphony.

Calling into question the form of a musical work amounts to something of a *j'accuse* in the context of traditional music aesthetics. The thinking goes like this: notions of form are bound up with notions of beauty, and by extension a musical work that is formless cannot have any part in a canon that is the embodiment of the musically beautiful. What is more, the firm belief that great art instills moral and spiritual betterment in its audiences has at times given rise to concerns about the harmful effects formless works may have on individual listeners as well as on the musical tradition as a whole.[1] This was an obsession in the later nineteenth century, when it became fashionable to charge one's opponent with the sin of "formlessness"—musically progressive composers such as Wagner, Bruckner, or Liszt were favored targets of this polemical strategy. Declaring composers' works formless was tantamount to intimating that they secretly enjoyed strangling puppies in the basement.[2]

The charge is predominantly rhetorical, and as such it can neither be proved nor refuted: any accusation that form is lacking can be countered by an exhortation to pay more attention. A more robust defense can go one of two ways. The fatal charge, first, could be parried with a fearsome arsenal of analytical or philosophical techniques to show how there is indeed form, but it is just harder to discern. And second, the more highbrow alternative would be to argue that any perceived formlessness is not a flaw but is by design—typically by gesturing toward the sublime, an aesthetic category that builds on the very notion of incomprehensibility.

Beethoven's Ninth, especially the last movement, was not above suspicions of formlessness. The early-twentieth-century British musicologist Donald Francis Tovey cut right through the controversy and put with characteristic brusqueness what was actually at stake when he declared: "There is no part of Beethoven's Choral Symphony which does not become clearer to us when we assume that the choral finale is right; and there is hardly a point that does not become difficult and obscure as soon as we fall into the habit which assumes that the choral finale is wrong."[3] Tovey effectively threw the ball back to the critics: it is not the composition that needs to pass muster but the critic's assumptions. If we, however, follow through the consequences of this position, it implies no less than that the authority of Beethoven and his work are beyond reproach; their rock-solid, immovable position is the very foundation of this argument.

Tovey's statement reflects in many ways the confidence of the early twentieth century, when the Ninth had been firmly established at the center of the musical canon. We would be less likely to encounter such ebullience during the mid-nineteenth century, when the symphony's position in the canon was still in question. A rare voice, whose cautious response effectively conforms with Tovey's principle, is this politely ambivalent American review from 1852: "Then came the last movement, about which I stay my pen. I did not understand it, and reverently stand in hope and faith, that its secrets may at some future day be revealed to me."[4] The anonymous reviewer frankly admits his incomprehension but assumes that the problem lies with him and not with the work. Both commentators, Tovey and the American critic, converge in agreeing that the question of form is inextricably wrapped up with the authority that exudes from the work and its creator. So what are the stakes of calling Beethoven's Ninth formless?[5]

FORMLESSNESS IN THE NINTH

Philosophical debates about the form of the Ninth go back to the nineteenth century, when emotions where running high and opinions about its form or formlessness were sharply divided. In 1853, the eminent Hegelian theologian David Friedrich Strauss, for one, did not shrink from calling the Ninth "monstrous."[6] He compared the symphony to a "human head painted on to a horse's neck."[7] This extravagant image is a learned reference to Horace's *Ars poetica*, describing something self-evidently preposterous. The problem of the Ninth, as Strauss saw it, is a mismatch between instrumental and vocal music, which both follow different aesthetic and formal criteria. Between the lines of his argument we can easily discern a rebuttal of Wagner's writings concerning Beethoven's work. To Strauss's great consternation, Wagner had laid claim to the status of symphonic music for the genre of opera—however improbably—and he had done so through the vehicle of the Ninth.[8] In Wagner's view, with the Ninth the whole genre of the symphony had reached the outer limits of its expressive powers, extending its metaphorical hands in a plea for help from texted vocal music. This self-serving historiography, laying the ground for the creation of Wagner's own music drama out of the Beethovenian symphonic tradition, clearly shaped Strauss's argument. Human voices, Strauss held, may never be an accompanying force; they are always the main focus. After three full movements of Beethoven final symphony, the vocal parts entered too late, in Strauss's reckoning, to maintain an appropriate balance, and, what was worse, the choral parts were the most banal part of the score. Is the Ninth a piece of instrumental music in which the human voice is downgraded to just another sound color?

Coming from a theologian, Strauss's controversial observations on the Ninth were easy to dismiss as incompetent comments by a dabbling outsider. But an insider, none other than the eminent music critic Eduard Hanslick, picked up Strauss's idea when he called the finale of the Ninth "a vast shadow of a titanic body"—not actually a part of the symphony.[9] At the time of his critique, Hanslick was laying out an aesthetic argument that was ill-equipped to deal easily with the entry of vocal parts into a symphonic score. The core of Hanslick's ideas about musical form, specifically the form of nonrepresentational instrumental music, boiled down to the concept of "rhythm on the large scale," (Rhythmus im Großen).[10] As he explained in his influential treatise *On the Musically Beautiful* (1854), this idea required that certain proportional durations be maintained in the formal parts, analogous to spatial relations in the visual arts.[11] How exactly this was fulfilled Hanslick left unspecified, wisely perhaps. He himself argued that the critical temporal unit was the theme, whereas others defined forms in terms of periods, harmonic structure, or preexisting formal schemes like AAB or ABA. The question of musical form, Hanslick believed, was especially pertinent in instrumental music, the genre on which he concentrated and that he had spent so much energy rehabilitating. It is against this perspective that the vocal finale of the Ninth would cause him such chagrin.

These aesthetic concerns about appropriate categories for vocal and instrumental music seem quaint nowadays; the bulk of modern literature has no qualms about interpreting the whole symphony in terms of instrumental forms. The question of form, however, has not gone away. Even within the realm of instrumental forms there are a plethora of options, none of them conclusive. Countless formal schemes have been proposed to understand the form of Beethoven's Ninth, and especially the final movement. It has been identified as a sonata form, a set of variations, a rondo form, or a Lisztian four movements in one.[12] Many more formal types have been suggested, and reasonable claims have been made in support of all of them, though without leading to consensus.[13] The only thing that can be said about the last movement with any certainty is that there is no clarity about its form. Does it then follow that the Ninth is a monstrosity?

THE MUSICAL NOW

Another mid-nineteenth-century Hegelian philosopher, Friedrich Theodor Vischer, located the problem of form elsewhere. Where Strauss and Hanslick pointed at features of the composition that were at fault, Vischer identified the issue in the relation between the music and the listener. He argued that Beethoven's symphonies, and especially the Ninth, were simply too much to take in:

> The content is too rich or too deep or too complex for its forms; the forms are not merely stretched out, but—as in the case of the final symphony—actually exploded. Music has reached the outermost limits to which subjective geniality grants access.[14]

Needless to say, Vischer was not aware of *9 Beet Stretch*, but his description matches the situation quite closely. Here the temporal forms are literally stretched out, blown up, to the extent that our attention span is insufficient to comprehend them. Whichever way we cast our definition of form—whether as themes, as phrases and periods, as formal parts, or in accord with other philosophical or critical traditions—the question of temporality is a central aspect.[15] But how does the notion of stretching time affect our understanding of the music and its form, however we conceive it?

One of the most influential critiques of temporality takes us back to ancient Greece—with its ideas of kairos (instant) and chronos (sequential time)—and specifically to the so-called arrow paradox, usually associated with the pre-Socratic philosopher Zeno of Elea (ca. 490–430BCE).[16] If we observe an arrow in flight, experience tells us that it will reach its goal after a short amount of time. Zeno argued, however, that the arrow is not in fact in motion. For motion to occur, an object must change the position it occupies. If we imagine the flight of the arrow as a series of instants, however, the arrow is always at one definite point in space. That is, at any given moment in time, at every kairos, the arrow is at one and exactly one point only. This means, Zeno's paradox concludes, that at any given instant of time the arrow is not in motion, and, more generally, if each instant is motionless, and if time is entirely composed of instants, then motion itself is impossible. Generations of philosophers, going back to Aristotle, wrestled with this argument. The instant and the flow of time are two ways in which we perceive time, but how can one be translated into the other? Certainly, before mathematicians in the seventeenth century worked out infinitesimal calculus (or, for that matter, before the 1999 blockbuster movie *The Matrix* popularized "bullet time"—the movie equivalent of granular sampling), the inability to mediate between the instant and the flow seemed very real.

In the digital realm, as we have seen in the cases of granular synthesis and 9 *Beet Stretch*, this transformation becomes possible. However, the important difference here is that an "instant" is not dimensionless, but just a very short duration of time, just a few milliseconds. Nature, as they say, does not make leaps, but digital media certainly do: digitized sounds are based on a series of discrete and momentarily stable states, operating below our perceptual threshold—the flying arrow hovers in the air for a fraction of a second before moving to the next point in space, constituting an (imperceptibly static) kind of "motion."

In such situations, what happens to the musical now? That "short duration of which we are immediately and incessantly sensible,"[17] the now is a perceptual unit that has created enormous headaches for philosophers of time.

A profoundly subjective category, the now is radically dis-connected from clock time. Now is best understood as the thing that gives us a distinct sense of being in the present. This is no small task, since the present moment is forever changing: it is only bounded by that which is no longer and that which is not yet, which is just another way of saying that the present is that which is neither past nor future. Going back to Zeno, it is tempting to define the now as a forever fleeting point in time with no extension at all, impossible to capture. But there is one added com-plication: we only become aware of now a few instants after the moment has passed—we notice the presence of the present only once we have recreated it in our mind. The Polish poet Wisława Szimborska marveled at this impossible now in her sublimely terse poem "Trzy słowa najdziwniejsze" (The Three Oddest Words): "When I pro-nounce the word Future / The first syllable already belongs to the past."[18]

As a psychological category, the now is eminently suscep-tible to time-bending operations. We all have experienced time as crawling painfully slowly or as flying by. Music is generally very good at projecting a sense of now, especially if we think of music as "sounds shaped in time"—or, better still, in its more radical inversion, "time shaped in sounds." The philosopher Edmund Husserl puts music's role well when he points out that we hear a melody one note at a time, but it is only our memory of what has come before and our anticipation of what will follow that actually makes it a melody.[19] The flipside of this observation is that each sound constitutes an "event" that helps us perceive a sense of time passing. Many kinds of music set up regular metric patterns, often strong downbeats, that allow us to discern a sense of meter, of tactus. Putting Husserl's observation on more technical footing, Christopher Hasty has explained how a sense of meter allows us to create temporal expectations that can be projected ahead—once a regular pattern of events is set up, we expect another event at the equivalent time in the future.[20] This is what we call a pulse. If a pulse in fact materializes, we find our expectations satisfied; if not, we are either surprised or caused to recalibrate our expectations. Either way, this principle allows us to sense time, with its dimensions of remembered past, projected future, and—as a result of both—heard present.

The "musical now" is, needless to say, inextricably bound up with attention. If the window of our attention span is exceeded, we will not be able to project a sense of pulse. It is not the mere presence of sound that counts but the sound *event*—that is to say, the fact that sounds change—that allows us to perceive motion and passage of time. (From this perspective, Brian Eno's "long now" from chapter 4 actually presents a perceptual paradox: if the ten-thousand-year clock did not tick only once a year but every second, it would certainly be easier for us to maintain a sense of pulse.) For a musical "long now," take the half-notes from the third movement, in example 5.1, in *9 Beet Stretch*. This passage can also be heard in example 5.1 on the companion website ▶. In the source recording under Béla Drahos, at conventional speed, these two measures last about ten seconds, and the stretched-out passage is extended to well over three minutes.[21] When "duration turns limp,"[22] in François Lyotard's poetic words, the musical now becomes distended beyond recognition. In other words, even where

EXAMPLE 5.1   Beethoven, Symphony no. 9, third movement, mm. 123–24. In
9 Beet Stretch each of the half notes lasts close to a minute.

ongoing sound is present, the absence of new sound events and the lack of a pulse are tantamount to a kind of silence.[23] The musical now remains in limbo.

THE TIME OF THE SUBLIME

9 *Beet Stretch* stages Vischer's aesthetic concerns about Beethoven's Ninth before our ears and demonstrates theatrically the music's excessive demands on our attention. But where some see a shortcoming, others see a virtue. From a perceptual perspective on time, such "sounding silence" and stretched-out sonorities may constitute a problem of form, while from a certain aesthetic vantage point, this scenario could be the hallmark of the sublime.

The sublime is beauty's supplement. It has traditionally been defined as "no longer" or "not yet" beautiful; where philosophical definitions of beauty generally build on ideas of harmony and balance, the sublime is characterized by excess and sensory overload. But the sublime is also an inherently unstable category, always breaking apart into multiple possibilities. Immanuel Kant, for one, famously differentiated between the "mathematical" and the "dynamic" sublime.[24] We can translate these into expressions of "too many" or "too much," respectively, building on conceptions of infinity or overwhelming force. Either way, the sublime describes a relationship in which, put simply, the perceiving subject is confronted with a power much greater than his or her individuality. The individual struggles to make sense of it all and, if he or she emerges victorious, may grow psychologically and philosophically from the encounter.

Arthur Seidl, a philosopher and card-carrying Wagnerian, proposed his ideas in *On the Musically Sublime* (1887). The title was not coincidental: it was intended as a broadside from the Wagnerian camp against Hanslick's influential ideas on musical form. Where Hanslick argued that all forms were ultimately "rhythm on the large scale," Seidl countered that the musically sublime came about precisely when there was no perceptible rhythm, in a condition he called "a-metric." He argued: "The more rhythm (in a stricter as well as in a narrower sense) retreats, indeed disappears, the sooner this 'musically sublime' will break through as the ultimate, innermost core of musical art."[25] Where proportions—determined by large-scale rhythms, that is, durations—articulated a form and hence a sense of beauty in music, the absence of such proportionality formed for him the basis of an experience of the sublime in music.

Needless to say, countless commentators, philosophers, and music theorists, have identified elements of sublimity in music, and many have pointed at instances of them in the Ninth.[26] Adolf Zeising was thinking particularly of chorales as sublime and identified slow tempos and tones in the low register as its hallmarks.[27] Hugo Riemann, who took his cue from the idea of transcending human proportions, singled out trombone and trumpet sounds, which exceed the capacity of the human voice, as well as slow tempos that stay significantly below the human heartbeat.[28] For Hermann Stephani, the intricate polyphonic textures of a Bach fugue were the epitome of the sublime in music.[29] Seidl acknowledged these and other attempts at a definition, but argued that they were ultimately based on musical representations of sublimity and stopped short of an experience of the sublime itself. He thought of these representational moments as fairly superficial (which he called "sublime-*in*-music"), and contrasted them with the more radical sublime-*of*-music, in which music espoused its unique temporal nature and *became* sublime.[30]

Seidl's aesthetics of the musically sublime is predicated on a distinction between spatiality and temporality. Rhythmic or metric regularities, for him, will always lead back to a spatialized, architectural concept of music that is not and could not be, in Seidl's understanding, in itself sublime. In order to attain the sublime, he asserted, music must leave behind all spatiality and fully embrace its radical temporality. Put differently, the sublime is the moment when we lose a sense of now, when we become fully immersed in it, when form turns into formlessness.

EXAMPLE 5.2   Beethoven, Symphony no. 9, third movement, beginning of Andante moderato, mm. 25–28. (Piano reduction from Seidl.) Seidl identifies a slow rocking motion in these rhythms.

The Ninth is, as Seidl explained, a "particularly striking example"[31] of what he had in mind. Seidl brings his readers closer to an understanding of the musically sublime with a close reading of the lilting passage from the third movement shown in example 5.2, which he described as a subjective sensation of a swaying motion around a center of gravity. The passage in question, starting a new tempo and a new time signature, avoids changes on the strong beat in multiple ways. The bass circles around a repeated A, a dominant pedal, which is suspended across the bar. The melodic line adds to this impression by piling up further instabilities, beginning with an F-sharp that is anticipated by an eighth note, which serves to shift the sound events away from the main beat. Seidl's exclamation: "It's rocking!" (Es rollt!),[32] invoking a swing or a cradle, gives expression to the physical sensation his hearing of this passage (and others like it) elicited in him. The swaying sensation he describes drew his interest because it pulled the rug of the form from underneath his metric feet.

Clearly, Seidl's hearing of the Ninth was indebted to Richard Wagner, and he cited various voices from the inner Bayreuth circle to further explain the "long breath"[33] in the slow movement of the Ninth, with its "drawn-out, as if never-ending tones, the violins lead the song" of an Adagio "demanding endless expansion."[34] Yet for all the invocations of a sublime slowness approaching infinity, the "rocking" passage does not quite leave the world of meter behind, as even Seidl acknowledged.[35] The regularity of its rocking motion can still create a kind of spatial impression, which would be opposed to the radically temporal essence of the sublime, as Seidl saw it. The epitome of Seidl's a-metric sublime is the famous *Schreckensfanfare*, or "fanfare of terror," the highly dissonant opening of the fourth movement. For him it was not the ear-splitting dissonance or the tremendous orchestral noise of this passage that made this moment special, but rather its rhythmic features. The anguished cry of the orchestra, Seidl explained, becomes sublime in direct relation to the extent its performance "eschews strict and measured rhythm and embodies something a-metric."[36] Seidl's impression here was particularly colored by Wagner's striking performance practice, as is captured in his retouchings of Beethoven's score. Wagner had decreed specifically that this passage needed to be liberated from the "tyranny of the beat."[37] Example 5.3 shows how he went about this task: Beethoven's use of the trumpet, which divides the music into short four-note anacrustic motives (♪ ♪ ♪ | ♩) would unduly stress the metric downbeat

EXAMPLE 5.3   Beethoven, Symphony no. 9, fourth movement, opening, (a) in Beethoven's score, and (b) with Wagner's rewritten trumpet part.

of the phrase.[38] Wagner's decision to fill in the rests in the trumpet parts, along with the other instruments, helps to de-emphasize the downbeat and to create the "rhythmic chaos"[39] that Wagner envisioned for this stormy opening and that is a hallmark of Seidl's musically sublime.

Philosophers have typically described the sublime as a mixed sensation. Edmund Burke's apt term "delightful horror" resonates strongly with the "fanfare of terror," in that it brings together elements of pain and pleasure, fear and triumph. Michael Chabon's reflection on the *Clock of the Long Now* from chapter 4 mirrors a typical pattern, in which the impression of overwhelming duration of the clock, approaching infinity, conjures up the insignificance of the individual lifespan, but eventually gives way to a sense of fortitude and confidence in the future. For Seidl, who takes his cue from Schopenhauer, the Wagnerian philosopher de rigueur, the experience of the musically sublime "lifts up the human from the individual world of appearances,"[40] and allows him or her to gaze down on the world—briefly—as it really is, lifting the shroud of representations. This dizzying sublime reality that unfolds before our ears offers a glimpse of a time without a clear sense of now. This conception is a far cry from Hanslick's orderly formalism of "rhythm on the large scale." Seidl's sublime formlessness is a time that blurs and wobbles.

CRAWLING ON THE PLANET'S FACE, SOME INSECTS CALLED THE HUMAN RACE . . .

We do not know whether Seidl's experience of the Ninth really lifts the veil of illusion to give us a closer view of ultimate reality. But we can put the experience of the a-metric Ninth in a wider context, which brings together certain aspects of the two options to rebut the charge of formlessness with which we started. We will do this obliquely, with reference to a famous thought experiment, in which the biologist Karl Ernst von Baer asked the newly formed Russian Society of Entomologists how we would understand the natural world, with all its processes, if our life span were radically shortened.[41]

Imagine living a thousandth of the average human life span—that is to say, about twenty-nine days (80 years = ca. 29,200 days)—while our metabolic rate is sped up accordingly.[42] In other words, imagine that the number of heartbeats over a human lifetime remains the same, but they are now squeezed into a thousandth of the timespan, and the number of individual perceptions between two heartbeats also stays constant—somewhere between six and ten. While the conditions are imaginary and to a certain extent arbitrary, von Baer assured us that equivalent conditions can loosely be found in the insect world. Objects that move too fast for our normal perception, such as a bullet, would suddenly fall squarely within our experiential world. And the majority of sounds would suddenly seem very low, oscillating into our hypersensitive ears as if they were a mere thousandth of their normal vibration rate. Most importantly, the frame of our observation would shift radically: sun and moon would stay in the sky for long periods of time, and seasonal change would be so slow as to be imperceptible. As this short lifespan does not quite cover a lunar cycle, we would not observe any regularity in waxing and waning patterns.

Von Baer's perspective on the perceptual transformation of organic nature opens a window that bears directly on the question of musical form with which we started. By bringing the question of scale into discussion, von Baer devises a dynamic system between observer and observation in which the observing subject's perspective is brought into play. Slowing down the Ninth is the equivalent of compressing a lifespan while preserving metabolic rate. It is this realization that allows us to bring together the diverse perspectives discussed over the course of this chapter. Going back to the critic's offhanded observation that *9 Beet Stretch* somehow gives us insights into deaf Beethoven's inner hearing, we are now in a position to counter: no; if anything, it is more like a fruit fly's hearing of the Ninth.

We don't need to be interested in fruit flies specifically to draw important lessons from von Baer's lecture. It allows us to get a better sense of how the music plays with our perception of what is "now," with our experiential window, and it draws attention to the sublime disproportionality, which cannot even begin to establish a relation between the structures of a sounding music that is orders of magnitude too slow for us. Both aspects are contributing factors to notions of formlessness. In this context, we can safely drop the dogged questions of value that are associated with charges of formlessness. What's left is the disorienting *quality* of formlessness. The problem here is not us, nor the work, nor—to counter Tovey—our attitude to the work and its composer, but the very disproportionality of our perception. It is the incommensurability between the rate of events and the limited frame of human perception that affords us this radically different experience of the well-known piece of music.

It may or may not be true that this experience—let's call it sublime—allows us a truer insight into the world, as the nineteenth century firmly believed. It undoubtedly allows us a more detailed-oriented experience of the music.

The fundamental aspects of this position hold true both for 9 *Beet Stretch*, the impossibly slow performance of the Ninth, and for performances at a more conventional tempo. The incommensurability remains—the tension between the musical material on the one hand and the listener trying to take it all in on the other. Recent approaches to the sublime have captured the process in terms of a power struggle between the individual and the overwhelming material that confronts us, with the listening subject striving to regain control—and assert meaning—over the totality of the experience.[43] In the case of the problematic musical now, the question is: How will we know what comes next?

The philosopher François Lyotard strikes a poetic note when he explores the terror of the sublime now, which he equates with a sense of "It happens that" (il arrive): "What is terrifying," Lyotard explains, "is that the '*It happens that*' does not happen, that it stops happening."[44] An ever-lasting now loses all meaning; a sudden silence could take us to the edge of the abyss. For Seidl, similarly, the sublime terror of the *Schreckensfanfare* resided in its craggy rhythmic features, which did not allow the listener to gain control over tempo or meter, and in the unendingly long breaths of the Adagio. The unpredictable temporality of Beethoven's music urges us to valiantly dive head first into unheard-of details, into the sounding material, into the phrases that challenge our sense of metric order, into the harmonies and disharmonies, into the noise.

CHAPTER 6

MARKING NOISE

A CRY CUT THROUGH the performance of Beethoven's Ninth Symphony. "A night watchman's song! No more and no less than a night watchman's song!"[1] shouted one of the agitated listeners during a final rehearsal of the symphony, just after the baritone's grand entry with the words "Freude schöner Götterfunken": Joy, beautiful spark of the gods. The cuss was a citizen of Leipzig, a town known for its stringent tastes in music and, presumably, the questionable vocal qualities of its sentinels. The weather gods immediately gave the lie to this disparaging comment: no sooner had the baritone intoned the song than the sun appeared in the sky, bathing the whole outdoor performance in glowing golden light. Another audience member at the same rehearsal, the organist Pfeiffer, turned around to object to the Leipziger's outburst. "Night watchmen,"

Pfeiffer corrected his fellow audience member while the music continued to play, "sing songs at New Year's. Here all the creatures of a planet enter triumphantly into a new millennium" (Hier triumphiert alle Kreatur eines Planeten in ein neues Jahrtausend).[2]

With this near-untranslatable hyperbole the German novelist Wolfgang Griepenkerl staged some of the raging emotions during a fictitious performance of this grandest of nineteenth-century symphonies, and in the process he also staged some of the aesthetic controversies swirling around Beethoven's Ninth Symphony during the early years of its long and rich performance history.[3] (Nowadays Griepenkerl's novella is remembered primarily for another moment during the same tempestuous performance, when a different audience member, the waggish Vikarius, noisily curses *Freude* as the "whore" freedom in disguise, which set off the myth that Bernstein would draw on in his 1989 performance at the Berlin Wall.) But whatever the diverging responses to the music, each audience member tries to make sense of the unwonted sounds they are hearing. When Pfeiffer admonishes the Leipziger for misunderstanding the symphony, his own interpretation of the music raises the stakes for the symphony to the nth degree, surpassing even Schiller's enthusiastic poetry in every respect. So monumental does the symphony become in Pfeiffer's description that its urge toward transcendence can only be described as compulsive. Not only does the symphony speak for *alle Menschen*, all humans, as Schiller had it, but even for *alle Kreatur*, God's entire creation. Not only does it mark the measly return of one year after another, as a night watchman might do on

New Year's Eve, but it marks the triumphal passage into a whole new millennium. The work, if we can believe Pfeiffer, can only be understood as breaking down and overcoming all boundaries—not only boundaries of time and space but even those between species. Only the largest possible quantities, unimaginable magnitudes, cosmic proportions, will do its sublimity justice. And we, the individual listeners, are minuscule before this larger-than-life symphony. But there is comfort in this sublime thought: we may become like lowly worms—or rather, like short-lived fruit flies— when we listen to the superlative music; the symphony will nonetheless speak to us, as it speaks to *alle Kreatur*.

There is a clear difference between telling the time and heralding a new era, and Griepenkerl's novella, which doubles as an aesthetic manifesto in multiple voices, reflects the range of perspectives that were brought to bear on the symphony during these early years, when the Ninth was still a challenging and controversial work that audiences rarely had an opportunity to hear performed. The fiery poetic criticisms that his boisterous protagonists noisily exchange during the performance clearly reflect a wide spectrum of mid-nineteenth-century sensibilities. As such, the novella is clearly of its time. But, no surprise here, it also appears far ahead of its time, resonating with the very contemporary, millennial issues that we have examined over the course of this book. The concerns voiced here, especially the concern with time, which appeared such a radical departure in the context of the extreme listening experience that Leif Inge's digital installation occasioned, had in fact been there all along. All that Leif Inge's "masterwork of a masterwork" did was to bring out, like the unheard-of dissonances becoming audible between the stretched-out chords, certain elements of the symphony that had lain dormant until the right light was shone onto it, or until granulation software was brought to bear upon it.

HISTORIOGRAPHIC INTERLUDE

As we wrap up the repeated sideways glances at *9 Beet Stretch* in this exploration of Beethoven's Ninth Symphony, in the service of learning to hear the Ninth with fresh ears, we would do well to embark on one final methodological reflection. The idea that *9 Beet Stretch* brought out features that were already inherent in the fabric of Beethoven's composition, that its role was to foreground and state with almost exaggerated emphasis certain aspects of the symphony that we associate with the sublime and with its monumental position within the canon of classical music, can be captured in terms of what the influential eighteenth-century encyclopedist Johann Georg Sulzer called an "empirical symbol." In his influential *Allgemeine Theorie der schönen Künste* (1771–74) Sulzer explained:

> If we are told that God created the world ex nihilo, or that God rules the world by His Will, we experience nothing at all, since this lies totally beyond our comprehension. But when Moses says: "And God said, let there be light; and there was light," we are overcome with astonishment because we can at least form some idea of such greatness; we hear to some extent words of command and feel their power; and if we are made to see instead of the mere Divine Will some empirical symbol of it then we are awed by its magic. . . . We must have a yardstick by which we seek to measure the extent of the sublime, even if unsuccessfully.[4]

In order to be effective, the sublime needed to avail itself of such an "empirical symbol" that would allow its recipients to grapple with the ungraspable. Sulzer's ideas stood in sharp contrast with the Kantian tradition, which we briefly revisited in the previous chapter, for which our very failure to come up with adequate mental representations constitutes a hallmark of the sublime. Sulzer approached the same issue from a pronounced theatrical perspective: the sublime object *stages* its own inability to be represented before our very eyes and ears. The "empirical symbol" allows us to gain a glimpse of what it means that the sublime exceeds our comprehension.

This theatrical approach is perhaps the chief difference between the "late-twentieth-century Ninth" with which we started and the "twenty-first-century Ninth" that we have been exploring here. The modernist sublime persists in its inability, in its failure, to be represented—what earlier we called the "big nothing"—whereas Lyotard's postmodern sublime, following Sulzer's lead, turns its very unpresentability into a feature, which is precisely what Huyssen captured in his anti-monumental monuments.[5] Perhaps the best way to distinguish between these two kinds of "nothings"—the modern and postmodern nothings, as it were—is by means of an old joke:

QUESTION: What is better—eternal bliss or a cheese sandwich?
ANSWER: A cheese sandwich. Nothing is better than eternal bliss, but a cheese sandwich is better than nothing.

The punchline pivots on the double meaning of "nothing" as the absence of something and as a something—a different *kind* of something—in its own right. Whereas the "late-twentieth-century Ninth" tried to train its listeners to *hear* the absence of meaning as a fundamental ambivalence, 9 *Beet Stretch*, as a paragon of the "twenty-first-century Ninth," turns this "nothing" into its gigantic meaning.

In 2007 the philosopher Slavoj Žižek, never one to shy away from a provocation, called the Ninth an "empty signifier."[6] In light of the many contradictory political uses that the symphony had been put to over the years, he pointed out that the symphony had become a "symbol that could stand for anything."[7] And, in light of the vast range of uses to which the Ninth has been put, it seems difficult to disagree. This is nothing other than the postmodern notion of nothing that we have been developing here—in Nicholas Mathew's bon mot, the Ninth is an "occasional work perpetually in search of an occasion."[8] The symphony's monumentality, as we saw, is in the first place based on its general meaningfulness; its specific meaning is created in each of the particular contexts in which it is sounded. We needn't think that this is tantamount to "anything goes," a blithe shrugging of the shoulders. On the contrary, it shifts the burden of meaning making from the musical object to the responsibility of the listening individuals or collectives. And, given the impossibly broad and contradictory range of responses to the sounds of the symphony during Griepenkerl's 1838 imaginary performance, all of which have some degree of validity, it turns out that this idea is not even particularly new.

This raises the important question of historiography. We opened this exploration of the Ninth with a nod to

David Lodge's *Small World*, with its provocative anti-chronological approach to literary influences. In the world of poststructuralist literary criticism, focused as it is on the textual encounters from the perspective of the reader, Persse McGarrigle's slapdash approach would be completely uncontroversial. But what we have been dealing with here, over the last few chapters, in our leaps between the nineteenth century and the present day, is not merely in the obvious service of defamiliarizing this all-too-familiar work. It is operating on the basis of an idea that is subtly but significantly different: the principle of recursion.

Recursion describes the "turn back to long-abandoned constellations of knowledge, which suddenly re-emerge as compatible and instructive [*anschluss- und aufschlussfähig*] on an operative level."[9] Adapted from mathematics and computer science, the idea of self-similar repetition often operates at different levels. Think of nested Russian matryoshka dolls, fractal Mandelbrot set images, or even sourdough filiations. Think also, of course, of the thematic recall in the final movement of the Ninth Symphony. This exponential existence, as though folded in on itself, is also a central feature of recursive historiographical models. The deliberately repetitive nature of this approach makes it possible, in the reproduction of apparent similarities, to produce and highlight dissimilarities. In this way, recursion provides a framework in which cultural processes and techniques can be understood, often by placing seemingly marginal phenomena—the "long-abandoned constellations of knowledge" from the above quotation—in a central position and confining central phenomena to the margins.

The model of recursion produces the kind of "non-simultaneity of the simultaneous" that some historians consider at the very heart of their historical project.[10]

This is precisely why the question of whether *9 Beet Stretch* and Beethoven's Ninth are similar or not, and the question in what ways their similarities and dissimilarities manifest themselves, has been so important over the last chapters of this book. The mise en abyme that *9 Beet Stretch* performs so admirably, by dramatizing the monumentality of the Ninth in all its cultural weightiness is both a sublime coup de théâtre and, simultaneously, a medial act of recursion. This is ultimately the reason that this "digital re-hearing" of the Ninth—which sounds nothing like, or at best faintly like, the music it is based on—can nonetheless tell us something important about Beethoven's symphony.

NOISE

We need not equate noise with the unmusical crowing of the night watchman that the Leipziger heard in the symphony, nor with the disturbance of the music by his interjection during the performance. As we have seen, noise has come to mean a whole range of things. To start with an oversimplification, music is what is in the notes, and noise is everything that shouldn't be there. Noise is disruption, noise is disorder. If music is that which is purposeful, ordered, and meaningful, then noise is never too far from nonsense. The best synonym for noise, in this context, might be a charming term, found in a nineteenth-century music journal: "unmeaning."[11] This is one of the reasons that Žižek's "empty signifier" caused such offense.[12] What if the Ninth has no inherent meaning that can be correctly deduced? What if it is nothing but "unmeaning"? If the whole symphony is merely noise?

Let's go a little further in exploring what we mean by noise. Remember from chapter 4 that this is one of the chief differences between the storage medium of musical notation and that of sound recording: the symbols used in musical notation, that is, the notes, invariably impose a "grid of meaning" that needs to be deciphered in musical performance and that sharply distinguishes between what is supposed to be there and what is not. The flipside of this distinction is that "noise" can be thought of as a stage preceding or existing outside of signification—it is that which cannot be codified in notation—for instance, scratching and popping on an LP record or static on a radio. From this perspective, engineers, philosophers, and musicians alike are forever seeking to optimize the signal-to-noise ratio, each in their own ways.

Jacques Attali, whose study *Noise* we encountered in the first chapter, took this idea one important step further when he equated noise with violence, specifically taking his starting point in the "non-order" that violates music's order.[13] The cacophonous opening of the fourth movement of Beethoven's Ninth, the *Schreckensfanfare,* or "fanfare of terror," that was so important to our aesthetician Arthur Seidl, springs to mind. But this terrifying sound is not the only notable noise of the symphony. As musicologist Robert Fink has shown in his painstaking analysis of Beethoven's score, the virtually unanalyzable harmonic progression of the recapitulation in the symphony's first movement, closer to discord than to chords, can finally only stand as noise. As such, it reveals itself as precisely the kind of violence that Susan McClary (and before her a whole string of mostly nineteenth-century commentators) heard in this very moment.[14]

For the French philosopher Michel Serres, finally, the concept of the "parasite" is has important sonic overtones of noise, with the French noun *parasite* having meanings of "static" or "interference."[15] Noise, in this parasitic context, denotes the parts that do not belong to the operative system, and more specifically that interrupt the system. But because of their capacity to interrupt, and in this way to point out the limits of the system, these parasitical noises are also essential in defining the system.

Sonic recording media, as we saw, typically do not distinguish between music and noise. It's all sound to them, as they indifferently engrave or encode the soundwave; the one thing that unites noise and music is their temporal existence. The media theorist Wolfgang Ernst updates Marshall McLuhan's famous dictum "The medium is the message" by further specifying, with a view to sound media: "Their content may be music, but their message is time."[16]

If time and sound, as noise or music, are inextricably connected, the responses of the audience—the interruptions—during Griepenkerl's fictional performance of the Ninth ring very differently. Where exactly is the noise, and where is the music? It all depends on one's angle. No one would likely argue that the audience interruptions themselves constitute music; without the performance going on at the same time, there would be no cause for shouting. The shouts, in a very literal sense, are parasitic on the music: they are part of the system, occasioned by it, and yet, in commenting on the symphony, they also stand apart from the music, frame it, and by this very act define it.

THE END

If we read Griepenkerl's novella further, we find that the lighthearted story soon turns dark; the noisy controversy about the Ninth turns into literal violence before long. In what amounts to a reversal of fortunes of truly (and self-consciously) Shakespearean dimensions, the chief participants and organizers of the performance all meet terrible fates, ranging from tragic to gruesome. For one, the passionate and irascible double bassist, Hitzig (literally, "hot-headed"), plays his heart out during the instrumental solo in the final movement. (In Beethoven's score, to be sure, this passage is played by double basses and cellos, but for dramatic reasons in Griepenkerl's version the music is crystallized into one solo part.) In the poetic logic of the novella, he has performed the symphony a symbolically pregnant nine times. Hitzig literally and figuratively lived to perform the solo, the first entry of the Joy theme, and this performance is, inexorably, his last. After the rehearsal, injured and drunk, Hitzig steps on his instrument. His double bass breaks, as depicted in Fig. 6.1, and so does his mind. Hitzig is brought to a chamber in a tower, for his own protection and that of others. His long-lost son, the incongruously puny timpanist Amadeus Hitzig approaches him there, in hopes of bringing him back to reason. But in a fit of rage the man-mountain Hitzig hurls the slight

FIGURE 6.1 Wolfgang Robert Griepenkerl, *Das Musikfest oder die Beethovener* (2nd ed., 1841), frontispiece. (Image: Mendel Music Library, Princeton University.) The bassist Hitzig destroys his instrument. Curiously, the timpanist, depicted on the left, does not match the detailed description in the text, which highlights his dwarfish, childlike features.

youth out of the window, and he falls, with a high-pitched scream, to his untimely death.

The image of Hitzig, a colossus of a man whose temper runs high, and his feeble, misbegotten, incongruous, but clearly loveable son, calls to mind the horrifying spectacle of the gigantic, bloodthirsty titan Saturn—or Kronos, "Father Time"[17]—devouring his son, in Goya's haunting, unforgettable depiction, shown in Fig. 6.2. Hitzig's final words, uttered just before the filicide, could not reference this horrifying

FIGURE 6.2   Francisco Goya, *Saturn Devouring His Son* (1819–23).

scenario more clearly: "You worm, sticking to my heel, flee, or my jaws will devour your earthly remains."[18] The raging Hitzig proceeds to destroy the site of the murder, the entire building around him, with his own hands. Eventually the roof collapses, burying him under the rubble. Griepenkerl's narrative leaves no doubt that Hitzig lived and died by music. He is laid to rest with the ruins of his instrument by his side.

Which is noise? Which is music? In the end, it's all about the timing. The crucial point, the kairos, is the precise moment in the symphony that occasions the heated argument in the audience of Griepenkerl's performance. And it is the precise moment in the symphony—again, according to the poetic logic of the narrative—that causes the sun to appear at the opportune moment when the baritone solo begins, when the instrumental music give way to the first sounding of the human voice in the symphony. Violence, interruption, unmeaning all come together at this point. But this clash also helps to clarify exactly what the sounds that each audience member hears mean. To some these sounds are a disturbance, an insult to our ears; to others they are a revelation. And similarly, to some these sounds merely measure the passing of time, while to others they herald the promise of happiness.

Should we hear this sounding now as no more than the croak of the night watchman marking a specific moment in time, or as no less than the eternal joyful sounds of all creation triumphantly marching into the new millennium? The choice is of course ours, and this freedom can be an awesome responsibility. We are meaning makers, composing our Ninths, somewhere between the poles of documentary correctness and felt authenticity, between history and memory. These Ninths may be a more pleasurable way to mark chronology than the ticking of the clock. Or they may grant us access to an ecstatic time that opens up a hopeful glimpse onto a glorious future.

ADDITIONAL SOURCES
FOR READING AND
LISTENING

T HE LIST OF RECORDINGS of Beethoven's Ninth
Symphony is far too long to allow me even to single out highlights. Perhaps two recordings could stand in for a whole host of others, organized in terms of time and bookending the whole spectrum: at one end is Wilhelm Furtwängler's 1951 recording (rereleased in 1999 on EMI Classics), and at the other Roger Norrington's pioneering 1987 recording (Angel Records) on period instruments with the London Classical Players. For those interested in statistics, Furtwängler's is not the slowest recording on record—Karl Böhm's 1980 recording with the Vienna Philharmonic lasts four minutes longer. But Furtwängler's performance, which inaugurated the newly reopened Bayreuth Festival Theater after World War II, is musically and historically more significant. Norrington's recording was memorably reviewed in Richard Taruskin's "Resisting the Ninth," reprinted in *Text and Act* (Oxford: Oxford University Press, 1995), 235–61, which has assumed cult status in the literature on the Ninth. As a matter of personal taste, I count Michael Gielen's Beethoven recordings with

the SWR Baden-Baden and Freiburg Orchestra, especially the later cycle (Hännsler Classic, 2012), among my favorites.

The literature on the Ninth is similarly vast. David B. Levy's *Beethoven: The Ninth Symphony*, rev. ed. (New Haven, CT: Yale University Press, 2003), offers a great introduction to the work and its reception. Nicholas Cook's *Beethoven: Symphony no. 9* (Cambridge: Cambridge University Press, 1993) offers a thoroughly historicized view of the symphony. Less strictly musical, and more explicitly political, are Esteban Buch, *Beethoven's Ninth: A Political History*, trans. Richard Miller (Chicago: University of Chicago Press, 2003), and David Dennis, *Beethoven in German Politics, 1870–1989* (New Haven, CT: Yale University Press, 1996). The documentary *Following the Ninth* (2013), directed by Kerry Candaele, considers the political significance of the Ninth in various parts of the world.

Readers interested in the broader cultural questions raised in this book will profit from Lutz Koepnick's *On Slowness* (New York: Columbia University Press, 2014) and Kiene Brillenburg-Würth's *The Musically Sublime* (New York: Fordham University Press, 2009). Anyone interested in finding out more about the media theory used here should take a stab at Geoffrey Winthrop-Young's *Kittler and the Media* (Cambridge: Polity, 2011).

NOTES

CHAPTER 1

1 David Lodge, *Small World: An Academic Romance* (London: Secker & Warburg, 1984), 51.

2 Ibid., 52.

3 See for instance Sanford Schwartz, "Eliot's Ghosts: Tradition and its Transformations," in *A Companion to T. S. Eliot*, ed. David Chinitz (Oxford: Blackwell, 2009), 15–26, and César Dominguez, Haun Saussy, and Dario Villanueva, eds., *Introducing Comparative Literature: New Trends and Applications* (New York: Routledge, 2015), ix–xi.

4 *9 Beet Stretch* can be heard, on permanent loop and in segments, online at http://www.9beetstretch.com/.

5 The definition of the digital humanities remains flexible; see Matthew K. Gold, ed., *Debates in the Digital Humanities* (Minneapolis: University of Minnesota Press, 2012), esp. 67–71.

6 Or, more specifically, a "medium writ large"—a discourse network in Friedrich Kittler's mold. See Sybille Krämer, "The Cultural Techniques of Time Axis Manipulation: On Friedrich Kittler's Conception of Media," *Theory, Culture, Society* 23 (2006): 106. Much of my discussion here is informed, directly or indirectly, by the work of media scholars in the orbit of Kittler.

7 This idea is not unprecedented. Karlheinz Stockhausen once suggested playing Beethoven's Ninth Symphony in one second; see his "Composing Statistically," in *Stockhausen on Music*, ed. Robin Maconie (London: Marion Boyars, 1991), 47. Similarly, John Cage proposed playing all Beethoven symphonies together; see Alastair Williams, "Cage and Postmodernism," in *The Cambridge Companion to John Cage*, ed. David Nicholls (Cambridge: Cambridge University Press, 2002), 237.

8 Interview with Johannes Kreidler, in "Time Deceptions," special issue, *Neural* 36 (2010) available online at http://www.kreidler-net.de/theorie/neural-interview.htm.

9 UNESCO, *The Information and Communication Programme* 24, http://unesdoc.unesco.org/images/0023/002321/232157e.pdf. A further plausible reason UNESCO focused on the score and not on the sounding music is the tough question of *which* performance, among the myriad possibilities, should be so honored over and above all others.

10 The complete digitized score can be seen on http://beethoven.staatsbibliothek-berlin.de/digitale-abbildungen/. A facsimile of the autograph score also exists in print, *Ludwig van Beethoven: Sinfonie Nr. 9 op. 125* (Kassel: Bärenreiter, 2003).

11 Stefan Weinzierl, *Beethovens Konzerträume: Raumakustik und symphonische Aufführungspraxis an der Schwelle zum modernen Konzertwesen* (Frankfurt am Main: Bochinski, 2002).

12 Marshall McLuhan, *The Gutenberg Galaxy and the Making of Typographic Man* (Toronto: University of Toronto Press, 1964), 31.

13 Pinning down "the digital" at the turn of the millennium is, of course, shorthand here. Bernhard Siegert's deep archeological dig uncovers the many strata of the digital realm in *Passage des Digitalen* (Berlin: Brinkmann & Bose, 2003), reaching back to ancient Mesopotamia.

14 See also Jonathan Sterne, "Analog," and Benjamin Peters, "Digital" in Benjamin Peters, ed., *Digital Keywords* (Princeton, NJ: Princeton University Press, 2016), 31–44 and 93–108.

15 Michael Steinberg, "Writing about Beethoven," in *Beethoven, Performers, and Critics*, ed. Robert Winter and Bruce Carr (Detroit: Wayne State University Press, 1980), 23. Nicholas Cook focuses this statement directly on the Ninth in *Beethoven: Symphony no. 9* (Cambridge: Cambridge University Press, 1993), 105.

16 Cook, *Beethoven: Symphony no. 9*, 100–105.

17 Maynard Solomon, *Beethoven Essays* (Cambridge, MA: Harvard University Press, 1988), 10.

18 Ibid., 3.

19 Leo Treitler, "History, Criticism, and Beethoven's Ninth Symphony," in *Music and the Historical Imagination* (Cambridge, MA: Harvard University Press, 1989), 19–45.

20 Solomon, *Beethoven Essays*, 23.

21 Ibid., 30.

22 Bertolt Brecht, *Der gute Mensch von Sezuan*, ed. Bruce Thompson (Bungay, UK: Chaucer, 1985), 178.

23 Cook, *Beethoven: Symphony no. 9*, 104.

24 Solomon, *Beethoven Essays*, 13.

25 Susan McClary, *Feminine Endings* (Minnesota: University of Minneapolis Press, 1991), 128–29. The original version—published as "Getting Down off the Beanstalk: The Presence of a Woman's Voice in Janika Vandervelde's *Genesis II*," *Minnesota Composers Forum Newsletter*, January 1987, 4–7—is more explicit than the revised version included in the book.

26 Pieter van den Toorn, *Music, Politics, and the Academy* (Berkeley: University of California Press, 1995), 38. The popular press reacted similarly; see for instance Edward Rothstein, "Musicologists Roll Over Beethoven," *New York Times*, November 26, 1995.

27 Van den Toorn, *Music, Politics, and the Academy*, 35–36. Likewise, the article version—published as "Politics, Feminism, and Contemporary Music Theory," *Journal of Musicology* 9, no. 3 (1991): 1–37—is more explicit than the book.

28 Robert Fink, "Beethoven Anti-Hero," in *Beyond Structural Listening? Postmodern Modes of Hearing*, ed. Andrew Dell'Antonio (Berkeley: University of California Press, 2004), 110–24.

29 Cook, *Beethoven: Symphony no. 9*, 105.

30 Richard Taruskin, "Resisting the Ninth," in *Text and Act: Essays on Music and Performance* (Oxford: Oxford University Press, 1995), 235–61.

31 See Theodor Adorno, "Late Style in Beethoven," in *Essays on Music*, ed. Richard Leppert (Berkeley: University of California Press, 2002), 564–68. See also his scattered remarks about the Ninth in *Aesthetic Theory*, trans. Hullot Kentor (London: Continuum, 2004), and in *Beethoven: Philosophy of Music*, trans. Edmund Jeffcott (Stanford, CA: Stanford University Press, 2002).

32 I take this image from Alain Badiou on Samuel Beckett; see Andrew Gibson, *Beckett and Badiou: The Pathos of Intermittency* (Oxford: Oxford University Press, 2006), 121–22.

33 Karl Marx's famous Eleventh Thesis on Feuerbach is included in *The German Ideology* (Basingstoke, UK: Penguin, 1998), 571.

34 Saheed Kamali Dehghan, "Tehran's Reborn Symphony Orchestra: An Ovation before Playing A Note," *Guardian*, April 6, 2015.

35 Peter Szendy, *Listen: A History of Our Ears* (New York: Fordham University Press, 2007), 36.

36 Jacques Attali, *Noise: The Political Economy of Music*, trans. Brian Massumi, (Minneapolis: University of Minnesota Press, 1996). See also Eric Drott, "Rereading Jacques Attali's *Bruits*" *Critical Inquiry* 41, no. 4 (2015): 721–56.

37 Attali, *Noise*, 137–40, 157.

38 If that is the case, Attali's fourth stage would be nothing short of prophetic, since the technologies that made these practices possible were barely on the horizon while Attali was working on his book in the 1970s. It is entirely understandable that Attali is very supportive of this line of interpretation.

See his 2014 talk "Music as a Predictive Science," available online at http://hearingmodernity.org/papers/music-as-a-predictive-science/.

39 This is the fundamental position of media theory. Especially pertinent here is Bernhard Siegert, "Cultural Techniques: Or the End of the Intellectual Postwar Era in German Media Theory," *Theory, Culture and Society* 30, no. 6 (2013): 48–49.

40 To be sure, there are some obvious differences. Szendy is ostensibly concerned with outmoded nineteenth-century practices, while Attali's fourth stage attempts to diagnose the present condition (or even the future). But Szendy's reconsideration of the act of arranging, which shines a spotlight onto a once marginal phenomenon and places it center stage, speaks to the cultural preoccupations in our own time, which are also captured in Attali's "composition."

41 Leif Inge's installation is self-consciously modeled on Douglas Gordon's *24-Hour Psycho* (1993), a seminal work of video art, which slows down Hitchcock's most famous movie to two screens per second, rather than the usual twenty-four. And Justin Bieber's "U Smile" was decelerated in 2010; see https://www.youtube.com/watch?v=QspuCt1FM9M. Predictably perhaps, this version, advertised as "800% slower" (a more attention-grabbing way of saying slowed down by a factor of eight), created a YouTube sensation and has been viewed millions of times.

42 See also Lutz Koepnick, *On Slowness: Toward an Aesthetic of the Contemporary* (New York: Columbia University Press, 2014).

CHAPTER 2

1 Eric Hobsbawm's *The Age of Extremes* (New York: Vintage, 1994) placed the end of the century slightly later, in 1991, with the collapse of the Soviet Union.

2 The article first appeared in 1989 and was expanded into a best-selling book, *The End of History and the Last Man* (Basingstoke, UK: Penguin, 1992).

3 Fukuyama, *End of History*, especially chapter 1. To be sure, Fukuyama is more interested in reviving Hegelian teleological history than the precise tenets of Hegelian philosophy, especially his notion of freedom.

4 Fukuyama, *End of History*, 41, 45–46, 86.

5 George Will, "The End of Our Holiday from History," *Jewish World Review,* September 12, 2001. The speed with which he found the mot juste, just one day later, is less surprising when considering that he had used this catch-phrase before, notably in his column "Clinton's Mark," *Jewish World Review,* January 12, 2001.

6 This event has been covered from numerous angles. See Esteban Buch, *Beethoven's Ninth: A Political History,* trans. Richard Miller

(Chicago: University of Chicago Press, 2003), 259–62; David Dennis, *Beethoven in German Politics, 1870–1989* (New Haven, CT: Yale University Press, 1996), 200–203; and Alexander Rehding, "'Ode to Freedom': Bernstein's Ninth at the Berlin Wall," *Beethoven Forum* 12 (2005): 36–49.

7 Leonard Bernstein, "Aesthetic News Bulletin," CD booklet for *Ode an die Freiheit: Bernstein in Berlin, Beethoven, Symphony no. 9*, Deutsche Grammophon 429 861-2 (1990), 2.

8 Ibid. Despite scholarly consensus that there is no factual basis to this story, this myth is not quite dead. Uwe Martin, "Im Zweifel für die Freiheit: Zu Schillers Lied 'An die Freude,'" *Germanisch-Romanische Monatsschrift* 48, no. 1 (1998): 47–59, is the most recent proponent of this legend.

9 Wolfgang Robert Griepenkerl, *Das Musikfest oder die Beethovener* (Braunschweig; Eduard Leibrock, 2nd ed., 1841), 206. We will return to Griepenkerl's novella in chapter 6.

10 This story has been told a number of times. See for instance Dieter Hildebrandt, *Die Neunte: Beethoven, Schiller, Beethoven und die Geschichte eines musikalischen Welterfolgs* (Munich: Carl Hanser, 2005), 222–40.

11 For the first version, see Friedrich Schiller, *Sämtliche Gedichte: Text und Kommentar*, ed. Georg Kurscheidt (Frankfurt am Main: Deutscher Klassiker Verlag, 1992), 410–13. For the revised version, see ibid., 248–51.

12 Buch, *Beethoven's Ninth*, 99.

13 Schiller's *Letters on the Aesthetic Education of Man* (1794) serve, in part, to explain his stance. He explains the changes to "An die Freude" in a famous letter to Theodor Körner of October 21, 1800; see Paul E. Kerry, *Friedrich Schiller: Playwright, Poet, Philosopher, Historian* (Bern: Peter Lang, 2007), 68.

14 See David B. Levy, *Beethoven: The Ninth Symphony*, rev. ed. (New Haven, CT: Yale University Press, 2003), 10.

15 Gail K. Hart, "Schiller's 'An die Freude' and the Question of Freedom," *German Studies Review* 32, no. 3 (2009), 479–93.

16 For a discussion of Beethoven's changes see, for instance, Andreas Eichhorn, *Beethovens Neunte Symphonie: Die Geschichte ihrer Aufführung und Rezeption* (Kassel: Bärenreiter, 1993), 229–33.

17 Dieter Hildebrandt discusses the worm in great detail in *Die Neunte*, 57–62.

18 Beethoven explicitly invoked the god of wine in his initial conception of the symphony: "—in the Allegro, a celebration of Bacchus." See Gustav Nottebohm, *Zweite Beethoveniana: Nachgelassene Aufsätze* (Leipzig: Breitkopf & Härtel, 1887), 163.

19 John Deathridge, "Elements of Disorder: Appealing Beethoven vs. Rossini," in *The Invention of Beethoven and Rossini* (Cambridge: Cambridge University Press, 2013), 305–31.

20 Pierre Nora, "Between Memory and History: *Les Lieux de Mémoire*," *Representations* 26 (1989): 7–24.

21 Esteban Buch, "Beethovens Neunte," in *Deutsche Erinnerungsorte*, ed. Etienne Français and Hagen Schulze (Munich: C. H. Beck, 2001), 3:665–80.

22 Nora, "Between Memory and History," 7.

23 In the wake of Nora's work, critics have stressed that the borders between memory and history are more porous than he was willing to admit. See, for instance, Wulf Kansteiner, "Finding Meaning in Memory: A Methodological Critique of Collective Memory Studies," *History and Theory* 41 (2002): 179–97.

24 It has been pointed out that the rise of Nora's memory culture coincides with a period of national doubt in France, epitomized in *l'affaire Papon* (1981–2004), which profoundly shook the self-image of the nation, especially the Gaullist concept of the *grandeur de la France*. See Jeffrey Mehlman, "Reflections on the Papon Trial," in *Obliged by Memory: Literature, Religion, Ethics*, ed. Steven T. Katz and Allan Rosen (Syracuse, NY: Syracuse University Press, 2006), 76.

25 See Jeffrey O. Seagrave and Dustin Foote, "'All Men Will Become Brothers': Beethoven's Ninth Symphony as Olympic Entertainment and Ideology," *Intersections and Intersectionalities in Olympic and Paralympic Studies*, ed. Janice Forsyth, Christine O'Bonsawin, and Michael Heine (London, ON: International Centre for Olympic Studies, 2014), 24–29.

26 Ibid., 27. The Japanese television company NHK came up with an ingenious solution to the problem of getting from low-latency (that is, a very short delay) to the unattainable ideal of zero-latency (perfect synchronicity): Ozawa was not conducting from the stadium itself but from a nearby concert hall. If he had been conducting in the stadium, the incoming recorded sound from the other venues would have lagged behind the "live" sounds in the stadium. This sleight of hand allowed the engineers to synchronize the recordings from *all* the venues, including Ozawa's, so that the audience in the stadium could sing along with the (slightly delayed) music without causing any problems.

27 See Eddy Y. L. Chang, "The *Daiku* Phenomenon: Social and Cultural Influences of Beethoven's Ninth Symphony in Japan" *Asia Europe Journal* 5, no. 1 (2007): 93–114.

28 Stephanie Strom, "The XVIII Winter Games: Opening Ceremonies; The Latest Sport? After a Worldwide Effort, Synchronized Singing Gets In," *New York Times*, February 7, 1998.

29 For vocal dissents, see Marta S. Halpert, "Ein Schlachthof ist kein Konzertsaal," *Der Standard*, March 3, 2000, and Marie-Theres Arnborn, "Eine Frage des Taktgefühls?: Beleidigendes und frivoles Spektakel," *Der Standard*, May 5, 2000.

30 That performance took place at the concentration camp Buchenwald on August 29, 1999. See Roger Cohen, "Israelis Join Germans in Concert at Buchenwald," *New York Times*, August 31, 1999.

31 Martin Kettle, "Ode to Joy in Mauthausen," *Guardian*, April 28, 2000.

32 Ibid.

33 James Schmidt, "'Not These Sounds': Beethoven at Mauthausen," *Philosophy and Literature* 29, no. 1 (2005): 154.

34 See Peter Tregear, "The Ninth after 9/11," *Beethoven Forum* 10, no. 2 (2003): 221–33.

35 Jindong Cai and Sheila Melvin, *Beethoven in China: How the Great Composer Became an Icon in the People's Republic* (Basingstoke, UK: Penguin, 2015), 117. See also Kerry Candaele and Greg Mitchell, *Journeys with Beethoven: Following the Ninth, and Beyond* (New York: Sinclair, 2013), 46–58.

36 See Cai and Melvin, *Beethoven in China*, 63–79.

37 Richard Curt Kraus, *Pianos and Politics in China: Middle-Class Ambitions and the Struggle over Western Music* (Oxford: Oxford University Press, 1989), 118. See also Cook, *Beethoven: Symphony no. 9*, 95–96,

38 The similarity with Romain Rolland's influential Beethoven interpretation and its central theme, "joy through suffering," was noted. Rolland was widely read in China (in Fu Lei's translation) and contributed much to Beethoven's popularity in the Middle Kingdom. See Cai and Melvin, *Beethoven in China*, 42–50.

39 Candaele and Mitchell, *Journeys with Beethoven*, 20–37.

40 Greg Mitchell, "Beethoven Leads Protest (Part II): From China and Chile to Occupy Wall Street," *The Nation*, February 18, 2012.

41 Ariel Dorfman, "Martin Luther King: A Latin American Perspective," in *Other Septembers, Many Americas: Selected Provocations, 1980–2004* (New York: Seven Stories, 2004), 104.

42 I thank Thomas Christensen, who was an eyewitness to those events, for this information.

43 See Cai and Melvin, *Beethoven in China*, 117, and Candaele and Mitchell, *Journeys with Beethoven*, 36.

44 Lewis Lockwood, *Beethoven: The Life and the Music* (New York: Norton, 2003), 412.

45 Rose Rosengard Subotnik, *Developing Variations: Style and Ideology in Western Music* (Minneapolis: University of Minnesota Press, 1991), 31. See especially the chapter "Musical Life" in Theodor Adorno, *Introduction to the Sociology of Music* (New York: Seabury Press, 1967), 118–37.

46 See Jane Donald and Gail Greig, "Orchestrating a Flash Mob: Reach and Reputation," in *Organising Music: Theory, Practice, Performance*, ed. Nic Beech and Charlotte Gilmore (Cambridge: Cambridge University Press, 2015), 262–69, and, more broadly, Darrin Barney, Gabriella Coleman, Christine Ross, Jonathan Sterne, and Tamar Tembeck, eds., *The Participatory Condition in the Digital Age* (Minnesota: University of Minneapolis Press, 2016).

47 See for instance, Aaron Shapiro, "The Medium is the Mob," *Media, Culture & Society* (2017), https://doi.org/10.1177/0163443717692740, and Susan Leigh

Foster, "Why Not Improv Everywhere?", in *The Oxford Handbook of Dance and Theater*, ed. Nadine George-Graves (New York: Oxford University Press, 2015), 196–211.

48 Available on YouTube at https://www.youtube.com/watch?v=kbJcQYVtZMo.

49 On Twitter at https://twitter.com/OliverSacks/status/635546050984574976.

50 An overambitious flash mob in Mainz, Germany, tries—and fails—to incorporate Beethoven's full counterpoint; on YouTube at https://www.youtube.com/watch?v=TSMCcT5lWfY.

51 This is even true on a less metaphorical and more official political level: adopted in 1971, Beethoven's melody for the "Ode to Joy" (in an arrangement by Herbert von Karajan) has served as the official anthem of various European institutions. See Buch, *Beethoven's Ninth*, 220–41.

CHAPTER 3

1 Louis Spohr, *Lebenserinnerungen*, ed. Folker Göthel (Tutzing: Hans Schneider, 1968), 180.

2 Mendelssohn was particularly concerned about the last movement. See Carl Wehner, *Ein tief gegründet Herz: Der Briefwechsel Felix Mendelssohn-Bartholdys mit Johann Gustav Droysen* (Heidelberg: L. Schneider, 1959), 49–50. See also Wolfgang Dinglinger, "The Programme of the 'Reformation' Symphony Op. 107," in *The Mendelssohns: Their Music in History*, ed. John Michael Cooper and Julie D. Prandi (New York: Oxford, 2002), 123. His reservations not withstanding, two of Mendelssohn's own symphonies, *Lobgesang* and *Reformation*, were clearly modeled on aspects of Beethoven's Ninth.

3 Andreas Eichhorn, *Beethovens Neunte Symphonie: Die Geschichte ihrer Aufführung und Rezeption* (Kassel: Bärenreiter, 1993), 93–123, analyzes the history of retouchings of the Ninth.

4 This anecdote seems to go back to the pianist Sigismund Thalberg. See Klaus Martin Kopitz and Rainer Cadenbach, *Beethoven aus Sicht seiner Zeitgenossen* (Munich: G. Henle, 2009), 2:983.

5 "Nachrichten," *Allgemeine musikalische Zeitung* 26 (July 1824): 441.

6 Richard Wagner, "The Rendering of Beethoven's Ninth Symphony," in *Richard Wagner's Prose Works*, trans. Ashton Ellis (Lincoln: University of Nebraska Press, 1995), 5:232, 5:241.

7 Ibid, 5:233.

8 Wagner's engagement with the Ninth spanned most of his artistic life: in 1830 he arranged the work for piano himself; in 1846 he conducted the work in Dresden in a widely discussed performance; the Bayreuth festival opened in 1872 with a performance of the work; and in the following year

he published his performance instructions. See Klaus Kropfinger, *Wagner and Beethoven: Richard Wagner's Reception of Beethoven*, trans. Peter Palmer (Cambridge: Cambridge University Press, 1991), and Nicholas Vazsonyi, *Richard Wagner: Self-Promotion and the Making of a Brand* (Cambridge: Cambridge University Press, 2010), 31–43, 62–77.

9 Wagner, "Rendering," 233.

10 Ibid., 243–44.

11 Eichhorn, *Beethovens Neunte Symphonie*, 123–35.

12 See Thomas Christensen, "Four-Hand Piano Transcription and Geographies of Nineteenth-Century Musical Reception," *Journal of the American Musicological Society* (1999): 255–98.

13 See K. M. Knittel, "Wagner, Deafness, and the Reception of Beethoven's Late Style," *Journal of the American Musicological Society* 51 (1998): 49–82.

14 Wagner's own aesthetics in fact allows for the spiritual kind of medium. In a letter to his friend Theodor Uhlig of February 13, 1852, Wagner explained that performances of Beethoven's orchestral works conducted by composers of artistic merit—such as Wagner himself—amounted to a direct communication with the great deceased. See *Selected Letters of Richard Wagner*, ed. Stewart Spencer and Barry Millington (New York: Norton, 1987), 251.

15 Carl Dahlhaus, *Ludwig van Beethoven: Approaches to his Work*, trans. Mary Whittall (Oxford: Clarendon, 1994), 77.

16 I have further explored this concept in *Music and Monumentality: Commemoration and Wonderment in Nineteenth-Century Music* (New York: Oxford University Press, 2009).

17 Thomas Mann, "The Sorrows and Grandeur of Richard Wagner," in *Pro and Contra Wagner*, trans. Allan Blunden (Chicago: University of Chicago Press, 1985), 134.

18 Andreas Huyssen, "Monumental Seduction," *New German Critique* (1995): 181–200.

19 Ibid., 199.

20 Available online at http://www.9beetstretch.com/.

21 Leif Inge clarified in an email conversation with me that while the presentation of *9 Beet Stretch* has often encouraged a mode of reception in terms of installation art, he prefers to think of it as a performance, in the sense that the continuity from beginning to end matters a great deal to him.

22 Practicalities played a big role here: as Leif Inge related in our email conversation, one reason the Naxos was chosen is that the label was particularly accommodating when it came to copyright issues.

23 An earlier version of the permanent loop had a different starting time: 8:15 p.m., marked as the time of sunset i23n Vienna on March 7, 1824, the day Beethoven's Ninth was first performed.

24 A precursor of Leif Inge's work is Steve Reich's conceptual piece *Slow Motion Sound* (1967), whose score simply consists of the instruction "Very gradually slow down a recorded sound to many times its original length without changing its pitch or timbre at all." See Steve Reich, *Writings on Music, 1965–2000* (New York: Oxford University Press, 2002), 26–29.

25 The emphasis here is on *successfully*; it was, within limits, possible to achieve the same effect in analog recording, but the mechanisms were extremely cumbersome. See William S. Marlens, "Duration and Frequency Alteration," *Journal of the Audio Engineering Society* 14, no. 2 (1966), 132–39.

26 Timbre recognition is a complex phenomenon, dependent not only on the steady-state component of musical sounds, which are easy to replicate and stretch, but also on the microtemporal fluctuations at the attack, the very beginning of each tone, not least because each individual sound event takes so much longer in the stretched version of the recording, the density of attacks, and hence timbre recognition, is somewhat affected by granularity. See Stephen McAdams, "Musical Timbre Perception," in *The Psychology of Music*, ed. Diana Deutsch (Amsterdam: Academic Press, 2015), 35–67.

27 Mark Swed, "Beethoven's Lasting N-n-i-i-i-n-n-t-h-h," *Los Angeles Times*, November 27, 2006; Ben Sisario, "Beethoven's Ninth Around the Clock," *New York Times*, April 11, 2004; Ingvar Loco Nordin, "Leif Inge— 9BeetStretch," http://www.sonoloco.com/rev/singular/inge/9beetstretch. html; Harold Schellinx, "9 Beet Stretch," http://www.harsmedia.com/ SoundBlog/Archief/00550.php; Kyle Gann, "Norwegian Minimalist Raises Beethoven's Molto Adagio Bar," *Village Voice*, February 10, 2004; Adrienne Gagnon, "Sound Affects," *San Francisco Weekly Calendar*, April 21, 2004.

28 Schellinx, "9 Beet Stretch." In our email conversations Leif Inge specified that his brand of ambient music is related to La Monte Young and Marian Zazeela's *Dream House* (1993) and is influenced, more broadly, by Tony Conrad and Pauline Oliveros.

29 See also n. 21 above.

30 Following the pioneering film theorist Rudolf Arnheim, Lutz Koepnick has recently made the case for slowness as an aesthetic phenomenon in its own right. See Koepnick, *On Slowness: Toward an Aesthetic of the Contemporary* (New York: Columbia University Press, 2014), 14.

31 Gann, "Norwegian Minimalist."

32 Swed, "Beethoven's Lasting N-n-i-i-i-n-n-t-h-h."

33 Ibid. The idea of imaginatively reconstructing what Beethoven must have heard is not new. Maurizio Kagel claimed his scandalous film *Ludwig van* (1970) tried to do just that. See Peter Szendy, *Listen: A History of Our Ears*, trans. Charlotte Mandell (New York: Fordham University Press, 2008), 140.

34 See Mark Evan Bonds, *Absolute Music: The History of an Idea* (New York: Oxford University Press, 2014), 285, and Michael Musgrave, *A Brahms Reader* (New Haven, CT: Yale University Press, 2000), 109.

35 Nelson Goodman, *Languages of Art: An Approach to a Theory of Symbols* (Indianapolis: Hackett, 1976), esp. 117–22 and 177–92.

36 See Lydia Goehr, *The Imaginary Museum of Musical Works: An Essay in the Philosophy of Music*, rev. ed. (Oxford: Oxford University Press, 2007), 21–43.

37 Goodman, *Languages of Art*, 186–87. The problem is that of the slippery slope: If we allow one mistake, why not two? If two, why not three or four— or indeed any number? For a stringent philosophical definition, the only option is to exclude any mistake at all.

38 Readers who like the anti-chronological approach introduced in chapter 1 can also turn this triple relationship upside down: the performance of the Ninth was designed to capture the CD recording, and Leif Inge's granular software was designed to capture such a recording (to capture the capture). Thanks to Jonathan Sterne for this suggestion.

39 Swed, "Beethoven's Lasting N-n-i-i-i-n-n-t-h-h."

40 This interview is available online at http://www.quietamerican.org/download/964/Idea_of_Ninth_7s.mp3.

41 Online at http://www.læyf.com/

CHAPTER 4

1 I have discussed this performance, alongside *9 Beet Stretch*, in greater depth in "The Discovery of Slowness," in *Thresholds of Listening: Sound, Technics, Space*, ed. Sander van Maas (New York: Fordham University Press, 2015), 206–25.

2 Due to fund-raising issues, the performance began in 2001, not in 2000 as originally planned, but the organizers initially forgot to adjust the dates of the sound events accordingly. See Ulrich Stock, "Seiner Zeit voraus," *Die Zeit*, March 31, 2005. The performance was adjusted in 2013 and will now conclude, correctly, in 2640. As an ironic consequence, Nelson Goodman would not have recognized this rendition as a proper performance of *ASLSP/Organ²*.

3 Jem Finer, *Longplayer* (London: Artangel, 1999). 44. *Longplayer* can be heard on the internet, on live stream: http://longplayer.org/.

4 Stewart Brand, *The Clock of the Long Now: Time and Responsibility* (New York: Basic Books, 1999), 2.

5 It is impossible to give a precise number because our calendar gets adjusted every few centuries—sometimes by papal decree (ten days were omitted in the switch from Julian to Gregorian calendar), and more regularly by

omitting a leap day every four hundred years. Further adjustments will no doubt happen.

6 Michael Chabon, "The Omega Glory," in *Manhood for Amateurs: The Pleasures and Regrets of a Husband, Father, and Son (P.S.)* (New York: Harper Collins, 2009), 253–59.

7 Brian Eno, "The Big Here and the Long Now," *Long Now Foundation*, http://longnow.org/essays/big-here-long-now/.

8 "Wie langsam ist 'So langsam wie möglich?,'" John-Cage-Orgel-Kunst-Projekt Halberstadt project website, http://www.aslsp.org/de/das-projekt.html.

9 Another timepiece, the Doomsday Clock, measuring the likelihood of global catastrophe, which has been hovering close to midnight for a while now, looms large here. See also Roy Scranton, *Learning to Die in the Anthropocene: Reflections on the End of a Civilization* (San Francisco: City Lights, 2015).

10 Chabon, "Omega Glory," 259.

11 This story is retold on the Philips and Sony websites. See http://web.archive.org/web/20080129201342/www.research.philips.com/newscenter/dossier/optrec/beethoven.html (this website is now no longer available); http://www.sony.co.jp/SonyInfo/CorporateInfo/History/SonyHistory/2-08.html. Thanks to Jonathan Service for his Japanese translation.

12 For a critical account that counters the official narrative, see Kees A. Schouhamer Immink, "Shannon, Beethoven, and the Compact Disc," *IEEE Information Theory Society Newsletter* 57, no. 4 (December 2007): 42–46. See also Jonathan Sterne, *MP3: The Meaning of a Format* (Durham, NC: Duke University Press, 2012), 12–15.

13 From an earlier version of the Philips website, no longer available, http://web.archive.org/web/20080129201342/www.research.philips.com/newscenter/dossier/optrec/beethoven.html.

14 Sybille Krämer, "The Cultural Techniques of Time Axis Manipulation: On Friedrich Kittler's Conception of Media," *Theory, Culture & Society* 23 (2006): 106.

15 See Sybille Krämer and Horst Bredekamp, eds., *Bild—Schrift—Zahl* (Munich: Fink, 2008). See also Geoffrey Winthrop Young, "Cultural Techniques: An Introduction," *Theory, Culture and Society* 30 (2013): 3–19.

16 Krämer, "Time Axis Manipulation," 99.

17 This is not to suggest that recordings are somehow neutral: their filter function operates on a different level. See Melle Krumhout, "Noise Resonance: Technological Sound Production and the Logic of Filtering" (PhD diss., University of Amsterdam, 2017).

18 Eric Rothenbuhler and John Durham Peters, "Defining Phonography: An Experiment in Theory," *Musical Quarterly* 81, no. 2 (1997): 243.

19 George Grove, *Beethoven and his Nine Symphonies* (London: Novello, 1898), 372.

20 Gustav Nottebohm, "Skizzen zur Neunten Symphonie," in *Zweite Beethoveniana: Nachgelassene Aufsätze* (Leipzig: C. F. Peters, 1887), 189–91. Stephen Rumph discusses the recitatives in his *Beethoven after Napoleon: Political Romanticism in the Late Works* (Berkeley: University of California Press, 2004), 195–221.

21 For further discussion of recursion see chapter 6 below.

22 This concept is explicitly modeled on the idea of musical experience. See Frank R. Ankersmit, *The Sublime Historical Experience* (Stanford, CA: Stanford University Press, 2005), 120–21. See also Wolfgang Ernst, *Im Medium erklingt die Zeit* (Berlin: Kadmos, 2015), 195–96.

23 Maynard Solomon, "The Ninth Symphony: A Call to Order," in *Beethoven Essays* (Cambridge, MA: Harvard University Press, 1988), 5–18.

CHAPTER 5

1 I have explored some of the implications of "musical degeneration" in "Unsound Seeds," in *Staging the Scientific Imagination*, ed. David Trippett and Benjamin Walton (Cambridge: Cambridge University Press, forthcoming).

2 With apologies to Geoffrey Winthrop-Young, from whom I am borrowing this gruesome image. See *Kittler and the Media* (Cambridge, UK: Polity, 2011), 121.

3 Donald F. Tovey, "Beethoven, Symphony no. 9 op. 125," in *Symphonies and Orchestral Works* (Oxford: Oxford University Press, 1972), 1:85. Note Tovey's subtle equivocation, "*hardly* a point," which provides a rhetorical exit strategy in case anyone mounts objections to his argument.

4 P, "Correspondence," *Dwight's Journal of Music* 1, no. 14 (1852): 109. See Ruth Solie, *Music in Other Words: Victorian Conversations* (Berkeley: University of California Press, 2004), 14.

5 Eldritch Priest offers a provocative reflection on formlessness in his *Boring Formless Nonsense: Experimental Music and the Aesthetics of Failure* (New York: Bloomsbury, 2013), 103–94.

6 David Friedrich Strauss, "Beethovens Neunte Symphonie und ihre Bewunderer," *Allgemeine musikalische Zeitung* 12, no. 9 (1877): col. 129.

7 Ibid.

8 Richard Wagner, *Richard Wagner's Prose Works*, trans. W. Ashton Ellis (Lincoln: University of Nebraska Press, 1993), 1:126.

9 Eduard Hanslick, *On the Musically Beautiful*, trans. Geoffrey Payzant (Indianapolis, IN: Hackett, 1986), 43n.

10 Ibid., 28 (translation modified.)

11 He made this argument so forcefully in order to rebut the powerful tradition in philosophical thought that held music to be excessively sensuous and lacking in form. See especially Immanuel Kant, *Critique of the Power of Judgment*, trans. Paul Guyer and Eric Matthews (Cambridge: Cambridge University Press, 2000), 205.

12 James Webster, "The Form of the Finale of Beethoven's Ninth Symphony," *Beethoven Forum* 1 (1992): 25–62.

13 Michael Tusa, "Noch einmal: Form and Content in the Finale of Beethoven's Ninth Symphony," *Beethoven Forum* 7 (1999): 113–37.

14 Friedrich Theodor Vischer, *Ästhetik oder Wissenschaft des Schönen* (Stuttgart: Carl Mäcken, 1857), 3.2.4:1146.

15 Mark Evan Bonds teases apart the traditions of spatializing and temporalizing approaches to form in "The Spatial Representation of Musical Form," *Journal of Musicology* 27, no. 3 (2010): 265–303. He notes that there is considerable overlap between both traditions. From the listener's perspective, as pursued here, the processual, temporal approach to formal unfolding is preeminent.

16 See Aristotle, *Physics* 239b.30.

17 William James, *The Principles of Psychology* (New York: Henry Holt, 1890), 1:631.

18 Wisława Szymborska, *Monologue of a Dog: New Poems*, trans. Clare Cavanagh and Stanisław Barańczak (Orlando, FL: Harcourt, 2006), 29.

19 Edmund Husserl, *On the Phenomenology of the Consciousness of Internal Time*, trans. John Barnett Brough (Dordrecht: Springer, 1991), 139.

20 Christopher F. Hasty, *Meter as Rhythm* (Oxford: Oxford University Press, 1993).

21 We may quibble about how long exactly the average attention span lasts. To be sure, there is individual variation. But there is no doubt that these sounds exceed any attention span.

22 Jean-François Lyotard, *The Confessions of Augustine* (Stanford, CA: Stanford University Press, 2000), 18.

23 Hasty, *Meter as Rhythm*, 78. On the idea of sounding silence, see also Ernst, *Im Medium erklingt die Zeit*, 31–32, and Rudolf Arnheim, *Rundfunk als Hörkunst* (Munich: Carl Hanser, 1979), 19.

24 Kant, *Critique of Power of Judgment*, 131.

25 Arthur Seidl, *Vom Musikalisch-Erhabenen: Ein Beitrag zur Aesthetik der Tonkunst* (Leipzig: C. F. Kahnt, 1887), 123. A recent reconsideration of Seidl can be found in Kiene Brillenburg-Würth, *The Musically Sublime: Indeterminacy, Infinity, Irresolvability* (New York: Fordham University Press, 2009).

26 See, for instance, Eichhorn, *Beethovens Neunte Sinfonie*, 256–88.

27 Adolf Zeising, *Aesthetische Forschungen* (Frankfurt am Main: Maidinger, 1855), 409–10.

28 Hugo Riemann, *Die Elemente der musikalischen Aesthetik* (Berlin: Walter Spemann, 1900), 61, 159.

29 Hermann Stephani, *Das Erhabene insonderheit der Tonkunst* (Leipzig: Hermann Seemann, 1903), 78.

30 Seidl, *Vom Musikalisch-Erhabenen*, 68.

31 Ibid., 127.

32 Ibid., 109–10

33 Ibid., 128.

34 Ibid., 127–28.

35 Ibid., 127.

36 Ibid., 119.

37 Wagner, "Rendering of Beethoven's Ninth Symphony," 240.

38 See Eichhorn, *Beethovens Neunte Symphonie,* 136.

39 Wagner, "Rendering of Beethoven's Ninth Symphony," 241.

40 Seidl, *Vom Musikalisch-Erhabenen,* 116–17.

41 See Stefan Rieger, "Der dritte Ort des Wissens: Das Gedankenexperiment und die kybernetischen Grundlagen des Erhabenen," in *Zeitkritische Medien,* ed. Axel Volmar (Berlin: Kulturverlag Kadmos, 2009), 61–80. I am grateful to John Durham Peters for pointing me to von Baer. See also Peters, *The Marvelous Clouds: Toward a Philosophy of Elemental Media* (Chicago: University of Chicago Press, 2015).

42 Karl Ernst von Baer, "Welche Auffassung der lebenden Nature ist die richtige? Und wie ist diesse Auffassung auf die Entomologie anzuwenden?" (1860), reprinted in *Zeitkritische Medien,* 45–60.

43 See Jean-François Lyotard, *Lessons on the Analytic of the Sublime* (Stanford, CA: Stanford University Press, 1994). See also Christine Pries, *Übergänge ohne Brücken: Kants Erhabenes zwischen Kritik und Metaphysik* (Berlin: De Gruyter, 1996).

44 Jean-François Lyotard, *The Inhuman: Reflections on Time,* trans. Geoffrey Bennington and Rachel Bowlby (Stanford, CA: Stanford University Press, 1992), 99.

CHAPTER 6

1 Griepenkerl, *Das Musikfest,* 206.

2 Ibid., 206–7.

3 See David B. Levy, "Wolfgang Robert Griepenkerl and Beethoven's Ninth Symphony," in *Essays on Music for Charles Warren Fox,* ed. Jerald C Graue (Rochester, NY: Eastman School of Music Press, 1979), 103–13.

4 Johann Sulzer, "Erhaben," in *Music and Aesthetics in the Eighteenth and Early-Nineteenth Centuries,* ed. Peter LeHuray and James Day (Cambridge: Cambridge University Press, 1981), 138–39 (translation modified).

5 For Lyotard the sublime is itself identical with the postmodern. See his *The Postmodern Explained to Children: Correspondence, 1982–1985*, trans. Thomas M. Pefanis (Minneapolis: University of Minnesota, 1992), 15.

6 Slavoj Žižek, "Ode to Joy: Followed by Chaos and Despair," *New York Times*, December 24, 2007.

7 Ibid.

8 Nicholas Mathew, *Political Beethoven* (New York: Oxford University Press, 2013), 192–93.

9 Ana Ofak and Philipp von Hilgers, "Einleitung," in *Rekursionen: Von Faltungen des Wissens*, ed. Ana Ofak and Philipp von Hilgers (Munich: Wilhelm Fink, 2010), 13.

10 Horst Bredekamp, "Wilhelm Pinders 'Ungleichzeitigkeit des Gleichzeitigen,'" in Ofak and Hilgers, *Rekursionen*, 117–24.

11 Anon., "A General Theory of Music," *Harmonicon* 10 (1832): 169.

12 Neal Zaslaw explains why he is troubled by Žižek's assertion in "Beethoven's Turks," *Musicology Now* (blog), November 24, 2015, http://musicologynow.ams-net.org/2015/11/beethovens-turks.html.

13 Attali, *Noise*, 25–31.

14 See Robert Fink, "Beethoven Anti-Hero," in dell'Antonio, *Beyond Structural Listening*, 109–55.

15 Michel Serres, *The Parasite*, trans. Lawrence R. Schehr (Minneapolis: University of Minnesota Press, 2007). See also Bernhard Siegert, *Cultural Techniques: Grids, Filters, Doors, and Other Articulations of the Real*, trans. Geoffrey Winthrop-Young (New York: Fordham University Press, 2014), 19–32.

16 Ernst, *Im Medium erklingt die Zeit*, 83.

17 To be sure, the titan Kronos and Chronos, as the personification of time, are different figures from Greek mythology. But the conflation of these two near-homophones is a time-honored tradition, going back to ancient times.

18 Griepenkerl, *Das Musikfest*, 244.

INDEX

deus absconditus *see* god
digital humanities, 1, 5, 30
digital age, 5–10, 23–30, 71, 74,
    78–81, 108
dissonance, 4, 76–77, 115, 120,
    123–24, 129–30
distraction, 56 *see also* attention
documentation, 7, 23, 33, 39–40, 59,
    69, 134
Dorfman, Ariel, 48
Drahos, Béla, 73–74, 79, 110
duration, 86, 97, 108, 110
    see also time

Eichhorn, Andreas, 68
Eliot, T. S., 1–2, 27
ending, 12, 15, 76, 84, 85, 132–34
engraving, 68
Eno, Brian, 87, 110
entertainment, 28
enthusiasm, 35, 37, 122
equality, 35
Ernst, Wolfgang, 130
eternity, 74, 120, 134
event, 43, 60, 75, 77, 83, 109–10,
    119–20, 126
expansion, temporal, 3–4, 71–74, 77,
    79–80, 85, 88, 101, 107, 109–10,
    112, 115, 124
experiential culture, 4, 8–9, 30, 40,
    45, 59–60, 68–69, 77

fastness *see* acceleration
Finer, Jem, 28, 85
    Longplayer, 85, 87
Fink, Robert, 20, 129
flash mob, 8, 51–59
form, musical, 6, 27, 29, 52–56, 61,
    75–76, 101–7, 112–14, 119
formlessness, 101–7, 114, 117–18
Foucault, Michel, 3
fractal image, 127

fraternity *see* brotherhood
freedom, 12, 33–35, 37, 40, 50, 63,
    122, 134
French Revolution, 35–36
fruit fly, 118–19, 123
Fukuyama, Francis, 31–32, 46, 57
    end of history *see* history
Furtwängler, Wilhelm, 73, 89, 135
future, 25, 39, 87–88, 104, 109–10,
    117, 134

Gielen, Michael, 135–36
global, 8–9, 30, 33, 41–42, 46,
    50, 60, 85
    village, 9
god, gods, 12, 15, 37, 43, 121–22,
    124, 132
    Bacchus, 37
    deus absconditus, 15–16
    Kronos (titan), 132
    Saturn, 132
    "Und der Cherub steht vor
        Gott," 37
gramophone, 73, 89, 90, 93
granular synthesis, 4, 28, 72, 74, 77,
    108, 124
green movement, 32
Goebbels, Joseph, 41
Goodman, Nelson, 78–79, 147n2
Goya, Francisco de, 132
greatness, 63, 68–70, 79, 123–24
Greenwich, 85
Griepenkerl, Wolfgang R., 34,
    122–23, 126, 130–31, 133–34
    Musikfest oder die Beethovener,
        34, 121–23, 31–34
Grove, George, 93–94

Halberstadt, 85, 87
Handel, George Frederic, 42
    Messiah, 42
Hanslick, Eduard, 105–6, 113, 117